The Sexu...

The Explorations in Feminism Collective

Jane Attala
Kythe Beaumont
Jane Cholmeley
Claire Duchen
Renate Duelli-Klein
Catherine Itzin
Diana Leonard
Caroline Waller

The Sexuality Papers

Male sexuality and the social control of women

Lal Coveney, Margaret Jackson,
Sheila Jeffreys, Leslie Kay and Pat Mahony

Hutchinson

in association with
The Explorations in Feminism Collective

London Melbourne Sydney Auckland Johannesburg

Hutchinson & Co. (Publishers) Ltd

An imprint of the Hutchinson Publishing Group

17–21 Conway Street, London W1P 6JD
and 51 Washington Street, Dover, New Hampshire 03820, USA

Hutchinson Publishing Group (Australia) Pty Ltd
PO Box 496, 16–22 Church Street, Hawthorne, Melbourne, Victoria 3122

Hutchinson Group (NZ) Ltd
32–34 View Road, PO Box 40–086, Glenfield, Auckland 10

Hutchinson Group (SA) (Pty) Ltd
PO Box 337, Bergvlei 2012, South Africa

First published 1984

Set in 11/12 Plantin, by Activity Limited, Salisbury, Wilts

Printed and bound in Great Britain by
Anchor Brendon Ltd,
Tiptree, Essex

British Library Cataloguing in Publication Data
The Sexuality papers.—(Explorations in
  feminism)
  1. Sex—History
  I. Coveney, Lal   II. Series
  306.7'09'04   HQ23

Library of Congress Cataloging in Publication Data
The sexuality papers: male sexuality and the social
control of women.

Bibliography: P.
  1. Men—sexual behavior. 2. Dominance (Psychology)
  3. Sex discrimination against women. 4. Women—sexual
  behavior. 5. Sexologists—case studies. 6. Social
  control.   I. Coveney, Lal.
  HQ28.S49 1984   306.7'088041   84-12867

ISBN 0 09 156971 0

Contents

Biographical notes

Lal Coveney is a member of the Revolutionary and Radical Feminist Newsletter Collective. She teaches in a secondary school and has been active in the Women's Liberation Movement since 1969.

Margaret Jackson is a lesbian and a revolutionary feminist who has been involved in various Women's Liberation groups and campaigns, especially Women Against Violence Against Women. Her particular interest is in the relationship between heterosexuality and women's oppression. She teaches at Goldsmiths' College, London.

Sheila Jeffreys is a lesbian and a revolutionary feminist who has been active in the Women's Liberation Movement campaigns against male violence, particularly Women Against Violence Against Women. She teaches adult education courses in women's studies and the history and politics of gay liberation.

Leslie Kay is an apprentice joiner and lives in Leeds. She has been active or at least semi-comatose in the Women's Liberation Movement for ten years and still thinks an end to male supremacy is a 'jolly good idea'.

Pat Mahony lives in South-East London. She tries to train teachers at Goldsmiths' College and her major interest over the last few years has been in the effect on girls of mixed sex schooling. She has two daughters.

Introduction

Lal Coveney, Margaret Jackson, Sheila Jeffreys,
Leslie Kay, Pat Mahony

The origins of our work

We are all revolutionary feminists. We met in the Patriarchy Study
Group (PSG), which started in 1978 as a support group for feminists
who were involved in research and who wanted to develop a theory of
patriarchy. The group underwent a series of changes in membership
and focus and, as we delved deeper into the question of precisely how
patriarchy worked to oppress women, we began to use the technique of
brainstorming around small and puzzling examples of male power in
action, such as gay male behaviour, male celibacy, and coprophilia.[1]*
We found ourselves continually returning to the centrality of male
sexuality as an issue, its forms and function in the social control of
women. As our discussions became more and more intensive and
exciting we began to meet more frequently, and for a period of about
eighteen months we met every six weeks for a weekend in different
parts of the country. We discussed our experiences in feminist
campaigns, particularly those against male violence, our research
interests, and our personal experience. Later, we began to investigate
what men themselves had written on the subject of male sexuality, and a
small group of us from the PSG went to talk to some gay men about
their ideas and sexual practices.

Sheila's paper came out of her research at Bradford University,
which began with the issue of the sexual abuse of children and
developed into an historical analysis of women's campaigns around
sexuality. This contributed to our discussions and was in turn refined as

---

*Superior figures refer to the Notes at the end of each chapter.

a result of the clarification of our theory. Margaret developed her research interests as a result of the discussions in the group, and our recognition of the need to examine the role of sexologists in the construction of male sexuality.

Pat, Leslie and Lal's work emerged from the difficulty we had in understanding the phenomenon of swinging or group sex: why should some men be so keen for their wives and girlfriends to have sex with other men? Someone suggested looking at *Forum* magazine, and what was uncovered was astounding. It confirmed the links we had been making between various aspects of male sexuality and the way it functioned to control women. We had reached the conclusion in the PSG that many features of male sexuality which were particularly damaging to women, such as the association between sex and violence, were being normalized by the sexologists; looking at *Forum* convinced us that such practices, as well as women's active participation in them, were being promoted as staple ingredients of the liberated sexual future.

A number of papers were produced as a result of PSG discussions, including those published here, which represent only a fraction of the content of our discussions, however, and cannot adequately illustrate the range and depth of subject matter covered in our weekends together. Nor can it demonstrate the tremendous impact of the group on our lives and thoughts. When we began to write down our ideas we tried various ways of working: some women wrote sections or topics on their own, which were then brought back for group discussion, or several women worked collectively, agreeing on the content sentence by sentence (as in this introduction) and then returning for group feedback.

Chapters 1, 2 and 4 were first presented as papers in draft form at a Women's Research and Resources Centre conference on Feminism and History at the Polytechnic of the South Bank in London in September 1981. As a result of this it was suggested that they should be published together. Chapter 3 was written about a year later and is included to provide a link between the discussion of Havelock Ellis's ideas and the analysis of *Forum* magazine.

Feminism and sexuality

The overall theme of this collection is feminist struggle regarding sexuality and the male backlash against it. The papers show how sexology and the ideology of sexual liberation have been used to subvert the critique of male sexuality developed by women in the 'first wave' of feminism[2] and how the sexologists' prescriptions for male and female sexuality have become the common currency of the contemporary 'sexual revolution'. Feminists today are fighting afresh to reassert the feminist critique and carry it forward, and we see our papers as a contribution to this continuing struggle.

In Chapter 1 Sheila describes how, during the 'first wave' of feminism, a massive campaign was waged by women (often represented by historians as prudes and puritans) to transform male sexual behaviour. They campaigned against the abuse of women in prostitution, the sexual abuse of children, and marital rape. The chapter describes the women's activities in the social purity movement, and the increasingly militant stance taken by some pre-war feminists who refused to relate sexually to men, in the context of the developing feminist analysis of sexuality. The main purpose of the chapter is to show that, in order to understand the significance of this aspect of the women's movement, we must look at sexuality not merely as a matter of personal fulfilment but as an arena of struggle in which male dominance and women's subordination can either be most powerfully reinforced and maintained, or be fundamentally challenged.

In Chapters 2 and 3 Margaret discusses the role of sexology in the construction of male sexuality and heterosexual relations. In Chapter 2 she argues that early twentieth-century sexology, exemplified by the work of Havelock Ellis, undermined the feminist challenge to male supremacy in general, and male sexuality in particular; that, in the guise of scientific objectivity, it constituted a powerful ideology, legitimating male sexual domination, and conscripting women into heterosexuality by means of a doctrine of sexual pleasure. Chapter 3 focuses on the 'second wave' of sexology, represented mainly by the work of Kinsey, and Masters and Johnson. It shows the continuity between early and contemporary sexology, and argues first, that it is based on the assumption that the heterosexual 'sex act' is a biological imperative, and second, that it legitimates male violence against women by normalizing sexual practices based on dominance and submission. Taken together, these two chapters suggest that the sexologists have constructed a model of sexuality which both reflects and reproduces the interests of male supremacy; in other words, that the particular form of male sexuality that exists under male supremacy has been 'naturalized' and 'universalized'.

The role of sexology in the social control of women also raises wider questions about the relationship between sexual liberation and women's liberation, which are explored further in the fourth and final chapter by Lal, Pat and Leslie. They describe what they found in issues of *Forum* magazine, the self-styled international journal of human relations, over a period of twelve years. They record how *Forum* has capitalized on Masters and Johnson's 'revelations' about female sexual capacity and popularized them in order to enlist women's enthusiastic participation in male dominant/female submissive heterosexual sex. *Forum* carries the prescription for women one step further by legitimizing hitherto 'perverse' practices and encouraging women to respond positively to such practices as swinging, buggery, bondage and beating.

As we have already said, one of the greatest difficulties in presenting our material has been the communication of the processes by which our ideas developed. This is frustrating because it is as important to us to record how we came to our conclusions and the effects they had on us as it is to publish what is for the moment our final draft. In the next section we attempt to make some of our ideas available in order to give a fuller account of our work.

Male sexuality as social control

What is social control?
In any political system of oppression the ruling class maintains its power and control in a variety of ways. There are economic and ideological controls to which social institutions contribute by different means. Behind 'soft' control lies always the threat of brute force. Police, prisons and the army exist in most 'democratic' societies to discipline those who present a threat to the maintenance of ruling-class power. As workers, women in capitalist societies are subject to the controls of capitalism: as Jews, blacks, and women of colour, women are subject to racist controls; as women we are all controlled by men. Under male supremacy, overt physical violence is used on a large scale by men to discipline women. For example, it has been estimated that wife battering accounts for 25 per cent of all reported violent crime (Dobash and Dobash 1980)*.

---

*Full references quoted in the text appear in the Bibliography at the end of the book.

There is one form of violence as control used in the oppression of women which does not occur in other systems of oppression. This is the construction and use of male sexuality as social control: through rape, sexual murder, sexual harassment in the street, at home and at work; the sexual abuse of children, 90 per cent of whom are girls (Jeffreys 1982); obscene telephone calls and so on, women are intimidated, constantly reminded that they are seen as inferior and punished for being women.

Why look at men?
In the PSG we became convinced that men must be studied if we are to understand and end the oppression of women. Time and time again in our early discussions about women's oppression we ended by talking about men. We do need to know more about what has happened to women in the past and more about our experiences now, but we must also study men, for it is they who are the problem. It is the institutions set up by men, the way men bond together and the way men act that maintain women in subordination. Moreover, men are not only a fit subject but also a vitally necessary subject of study for women. If we ignore men then the process by which we remain oppressed appears mysterious; it could even seem to be our fault.

While studying men we became more and more aware of the centrality of sex and increasingly puzzled about a vast range of what appeared to us to be highly bizarre practices. Why, for example, would some men visit prostitutes in order to eat their excreta from teaspoons? We found that when looked at from the point of view of how the social construction of male sexuality functions in the social control of women, this and other practices which have puzzled the 'experts' for centuries, became perfectly understandable. The 'perversions', which showed the desire to dominate, degrade and humiliate women, the disgust and fear of women implicit in what we read, were clearly only extreme forms of what was inherent in normal male sexuality.[3] Again, various features of male homosexual behaviour led us to think it was necessary to examine the ways men relate to each other when ostensibly (though not in fact) outside the system of power relations between the sexes. Male bonding, the hierarchies men create between themselves and the ways they express their sexuality with each other have repercussions for women: though women are not directly involved, dominant modes of male sexuality are nevertheless actively maintained and promoted rather than challenged by gay men.

'Normal' male sexuality – its characteristics

Feminists have long recognized that aggression and the 'need' to dominate form a routine part of what is accepted as male sexuality.

In as much as the exercise of male sexuality controls women, it is no accident that it takes the form it does. Male sexuality is not constructed as a mere reflection of the fact that men have power over women, but rather it is constructed and reproduced as an instrument of male control. The aspects of male sexuality outlined below are each perfectly attuned to the exercise of control through some form of sexual harassment or abuse of women. Not every man demonstrates each one of these aspects; but many men demonstrate some of them and all men benefit from the power conferred on them as a group.

Power
The need to dominate and exercise power in sexual activity is the basic common denominator of all those aspects of male sexuality described here. In the 'normal' male it is reflected in the expectation that he will take sexual initiatives: in the selection of sexual partners smaller or younger than himself; in his preference for sexual positions in which he is in control and the female vulnerable. In its extreme form the construction of male sexuality and its relationship to power is revealed by the selection of children as sexual partners and in much of the brutality, degradation and infliction of pain which will be mentioned below. Somewhere between normal and extreme, power manifests itself in many forms of harassment of women, such as sexual gestures, innuendoes, jokes and remarks which remind women of their vulnerability and subordinate status as sex objects.

Aggression
The aggressive aspect of male sexuality can be seen in all those activities which are aimed at making women feel uncomfortable, humiliated, physically disadvantaged or in pain. One example is the use of phrases such as 'What she needs is a good fuck' about any woman who shows insufficient respect for male authority or who is thought to be in need of punishment. Another is the pleasure men take in watching films and

videos which show women being raped, murdered or cruelly mutilated such as 'Dressed to Kill' and 'He Knows You're Alone'. Yet another is men's standard indulgence in rape fantasies and pornographic literature devoted to the portrayal of women as legitimate targets of male violence.

The most extreme form of aggressive male sexuality manifests itself in the rape and murder of women. It also facilitates other less overtly brutal forms of abuse in which women's bodies are used by men to achieve sexual gratification. In obscene telephone calls, hatred of and aggression towards women are made very clear.

Penis orientation
As well as being used as a weapon the penis is also the symbol of a man's membership of the group holding power and it is not at all surprising that he should focus the bulk of his satisfaction and sexual activity on this organ. Thus the dominant view of what counts as 'having sex' involves penetration of the vagina by the penis. Very many issues of *Forum* magazine from 1968–81 (156 in all) contain a survey of length, breadth and width of penises in different parts of the country!

An extreme form of this aspect of male sexuality might be the belief of most male-to-female transsexuals that penectomy is sufficient to make them no longer men. The commonest form of sexual harassment arising from penis orientation is indecent exposure or exhibitionism in which men try to impress, intimidate or humiliate women. They may be showing their authority much as a plain clothes policeman might 'flash' his identity card.

The separation of sex from loving emotion
This aspect of male sexuality was central to the 'sexual revolution' of the 1960s and was actively promoted as a desirable development for female sexuality. Sex with strangers, sex with prostitutes, one-night stands and male homosexual cottaging are all examples. Men speak of the difficulty of engaging in coitus when they are in touch with loving emotions (Snodgrass 1977). Being soft and vulnerable is the very antithesis to what is necessary to achieve and sustain erection so that they may have to resort to pornographic fantasy or to asking their partners to 'play the whore'. This requires that men develop the ability to objectify women.

Objectification
As an aspect common to many varieties of male sexual behaviour, objectification is expressed, as we have said, in the difficulty men experience in responding sexually to women whom they feel to be fully sentient and equal human beings. The solution is to set a distance between themselves and their sexual partners by turning them into an object, a thing which requires neither respect nor sensitive understanding. The ability of men to treat women as objects is evidenced by the size of the pornography industry and the content of advertisements in which women are reduced to objects and then consumed.

Extreme forms of objectification include necrophilia and dehumanization of women in bondage equipment which is on sale on many high streets. In both these forms of behaviour, women are reduced to total helplessness and non-humanness. More commonly, objectification is evidenced in appraising looks, whistling, shouting lewd comments and 'touching up' in which women are reduced to the status of objects for the judgement of men.

Fetishism
In this aspect of male sexual behaviour which is based on objectification, men gain satisfaction from parts of women or items of women's clothing, separate from the whole woman. In its most common form we see parts of women used in advertising, usually breasts, legs and buttocks. Men boast of their interest in parts of women – 'I'm a legs man' and report being excited by the sight of women in crippling shoes or clothes which emphasize hips, buttocks or breasts.

In its most extreme form, fetishism can be carried to the lengths of murder and dismemberment of women or to an inability to gain sexual satisfaction from anything but one tiny detail of a woman's apparel (as in shoe fetishism, ejaculating into a woman's shoe). The effect of fetishism upon women is that we are pressured to wear stylized clothing like corsets and high-heeled shoes which restrict our freedom of movement, diminish our self-confidence and cause permanent damage to our bodies.

Uncontrollability
Men are brought up to regard their sexuality as uncontrollable and to fear ill-health or some unspecified disaster if they cannot gain sexual satisfaction whenever aroused. The problem is exacerbated by the fact

that they are encouraged to find a wide variety of stimuli arousing. These problems are demonstrated in the enormous pressure put on women to sexually service men, and on men to seek sexual outlet at the least evidence of sexual arousal. This leads to a quantitative approach to sexuality – gaining a sexual conquest is described as 'scoring'. Power is also involved quite explicitly here. Within this whole construction of male sexuality, if sex is aimed at conquest, then a woman who allows sexual contact has been conquered, whether this is how she feels about it or not. For the man the more sexual conquests, the more powerful he is.

The argument of uncontrollability, however absurd (men do not become uncontrollable in Woolworths or Harrods), is used by police, courts and psychiatrists as well as by individual men to excuse them from any responsibility for the sexual abuse of women.

Sex and male identity

Ethel Spector Person (1980), an American feminist psychoanalyst, suggests that we should see what is considered to be a high sex drive in men as compulsive sexuality. She argues that men feel driven to 'act out sexually' because that is how they assure themselves of their identity as men. The question for us is, why should this particular identity be so crucial unless it serves their interests as men? We suggest that this identity, or compulsive sexuality, does serve men's interests because it functions to control women.

The social control of women

Women's lives and opportunities are restricted by the exercise of male sexuality in virtually every sphere of life.

On the street

Sexual harassment of women on the street can take the form of whistles, catcalls, comments, touching up, rape, kerb crawling, following, indecent exposure and physical violence. All these forms of male behaviour serve to remind women that men are powerful. They undermine women's confidence and self-esteem, they remind us of our vulnerability and of the necessity to continue to adopt survival strategies. We are careful not to look directly at men in groups, to keep our eyes lowered when in tube trains. At night we may walk in fear or at least aware of the footsteps behind us. For many women the fear and threat of rape are sufficient to keep them indoors at night in what they think is the safety of their own homes.

On the street and in public places we must also face the use of women's bodies to advertise goods, on record, book and magazine covers and on advertisements for films and newspapers. Such images remind us of our status as objects, as decoration, as bodies. As we grow up with them we may be unaware of the extent to which we internalize ideas of ourselves as sexual objects and how this structures our sense of ourselves as inferior and as worthy of contempt.

In the home
In the home women are subject to sexual abuse from two directions. Some are abused – even murdered – by husbands, lovers, fathers, brothers and other male relatives; we are all vulnerable to abuse from outsiders. Intruders, peeping toms and obscene telephone callers all shatter our security in our home. Each individual woman does not have to experience directly any of these to know that they are all potential dangers. Hardly a week goes by when we are not reminded of our vulnerability by news reports of women and girls being assaulted or murdered. Also at home many women have to exist in the presence of pornography in magazines or on video used by men in the family. On the television we are the constant butt of sexual jokes and innuendo; from newspapers, images of ourselves as pin-ups may adorn the kitchen table along with the toast.

At work
Sexual harassment of women at work is carried out by workmates and employers as well as by those we service – clients, pupils, patients, customers. It can take many forms, ranging from sexual jokes and comments to physical assault, unwanted touch, rape and forced sexual servicing. The most common jobs for women are those which are an extension of our 'natural' role of looking after others. Indeed in some jobs (such as bar work) the acceptance of harassment is almost a necessary qualification for the job. Women who do not accept their role to be sexually pleasing to men may gain reputations for being 'difficult' to work with, get bad reports and lose promotion, or even their jobs, if they refuse to provide sexual servicing to employers. Thus, sexual

harassment functions to undermine the confidence and efficiency of female workers, to depress our position in the workforce (MacKinnon 1979) and to keep us out of jobs which have traditionally been male preserves, such as engineering, building and taxi driving (two women taxi drivers were raped in Scotland in 1982).

Social life
An area in which harassment restricts our lives and opportunities and encourages us into the 'protection' of individual men to escape the harassment of others, is that of entertainment and social life. Women not in the company of men will receive a great deal of unwanted attention, some of which is violent. At the very least, comments like 'What are you girls doing on your own?' – directed at a *group* of women – are not uncommon in pubs. Many women feel uncomfortable about going into a pub with another woman, and few would venture in on their own.

Male sexuality, heterosexuality and male power

These are just some examples of the way that the exercise of this form of male sexuality functions to control women: by confining us in terms of the space we may move in, by dictating the way we look, by restricting the work we do and how and when we do it (female social workers think twice about where they arrange their evening visits), and by constraining the social life we engage in. The effect is to undermine our confidence and reinforce our inferior status, to alienate us from our bodies, and to induce a timid and careful response to men. At a more general level the exercise of male sexuality helps to structure and maintain our subordination to men, by pressurizing us into seeking the 'protection' of one man from the rest. Thus, not only are most of us forced into economic dependence on men: active heterosexuality is also enforced, which in turn leads most of us to 'choose' marriage, motherhood and the family, where the work we do further increases the power and status of men.

How is male sexuality acquired?

Something we have been careful to stress throughout is our belief that male sexuality is socially constructed, *not* biologically determined. We agree up to a point with sociologists such as Gagnon and Simon (1973) and Stevi Jackson (1978) that the way sexuality is experienced and acted out is socially scripted. The way little boys learn to act towards women and girls is partly the result of social influences such as education, the media, parental expectation and peer group pressure, but also partly the result of realizing, consciously or unconsciously, how their best interests are served. It is in respect of this latter idea that we would disagree with the majority of sociological analyses which depend upon ideas of conditioning, sexual scripting or socialization: all these notions lack a concept of power which is central to our thesis. Male identity and sexuality, as long as they are bound up with power, cannot but have a damaging effect on those who stand in a relationship of relative powerlessness – women. Put another way, men either individually or as a group cannot have power in the abstract, they must have power *over* someone: they cannot have authority if they do not have it over someone; they cannot have higher status unless there is someone in relation to whom they are higher.

So when men act in 'male' ways they are not just the puppets of their childhood socialization. They are acting in ways which bring them positive advantages in status, ego, authority and servicing performed: every gain for men is a loss for women. Into this analysis fits our theory of male sexuality as social control, where men themselves are actively involved in its construction.

Recent research into the sexual harassment of girls in school clearly illustrates how skilful boys are, at a relatively young age, at the practice of gaining power over girls (Mahony, 1983). Often when a girl attempts to speak in a mixed-sex class she is silenced by the boys. Often a half whispered remark (usually having a sexual content) from one boy to another is sufficient to destroy her concentration and to render her self-conscious and embarrassed. Often she will not be inclined to take a public part in the rest of the lesson. The boy responsible for the harassment does not just gain greater space for himself to speak but for all boys. This is because not just one girl is humiliated into silence but rather that all girls in being girls are equally vulnerable to similar comments. His gain is not just her loss: her humiliation affects all girls to the benefit of all boys so that in a class of thirty children, fifteen have been knocked out of the competition for teacher attention. Further-more, boys who do not manifest sufficient evidence of masculinity or, more rarely, boys who actively challenge the 'sexist' behaviour of their peers are prime targets for a good deal of bullying. Therefore it is doubly in their interest to adopt 'normal' patterns of male behaviour.

To say that male sexuality is socially constructed is also to acknowledge that it can be changed. It is as part of this struggle that feminist teachers are challenging sexual harassment of themselves and girls by male teachers and boys, and that many of the campaigns in the women's movement past and present have been organized. It is also in the context of this struggle that this book has been written.

Notes

1   Cophrophilia: marked interest in excrement, use of faeces or filth for sexual excitement (*Webster's Dictionary*).
2   The 'first wave' of feminism is impossible to date precisely. For a discussion of this problem see Sarah 1982.
3   For further discussion of this point see the article by Jackson 1981 which was also based on discussions in the PSG.

1 'Free from all uninvited touch of man': women's campaigns around sexuality, 1880–1914*

Sheila Jeffreys

The period 1880–1914 witnessed a massive campaign by women to transform male sexual behaviour and to protect women from the effects of damaging forms of male sexuality. There is, however, little or no reference to this campaign in the histories of the women's movement in Britain. Other aspects of the feminist struggle – such as the suffrage campaign, the movement to improve women's education and work opportunities, and to gain changes in the marriage law – have all received attention, yet when historians have mentioned the work of the same feminist campaigners in the area of sexuality they have represented them as prudes and puritans, have criticized them for not embracing the goal of sexual freedom or women's sexual pleasure and have found in their writings a source of useful humorous material (Rover, 1970, p. 2). While their activities and demands have been seen as challenging and progressive in other areas, the activities of the very same women in the area of sexuality have been seen as backward and retrogressive.

As it is not possible in this chapter to cover the complete range of activities and ideas of these women campaigners; examples have been selected to give an idea of the size and scope of the campaign and the motivations of the women involved. The women's work will be divided into three sections. First, I will describe the efforts of some women to protect other women and female children from the damaging effects of male sexual behaviour, in the form of the use of prostitutes and the sexual abuse of children, in the social purity movement of the 1880s and

*This chapter was first published in *Women's Studies International Forum*, 5 no.6 (1982).

the 1890s. These women sought directly to challenge and set limits to male sexual behaviour as well as to support the victims. Second, I will describe the ideas and activities of some 1890s feminists who tackled the problem of sexual behaviour within marriage as well as outside and sought to explain the origins and workings of what they saw to be the foundation of women's oppression, the sex slavery of women. Last, I will look at the work of some pre-First World War feminists who went so far as to promote the complete withdrawal of women from sexual relations with men in order to eliminate sex slavery.

There are certain basic assumptions underlying the work of historians on the history of sexuality which must be overturned if the significance of the women's campaigns is to be understood. The most pervasive is the assumption that the last hundred years represents a story of progress from the darkness of Victorian prudery towards the light of sexual freedom (Stone, 1977, p. 658). Implicit in this view is the idea that there is an essence of sexuality which, though 'repressed' at time in the past, is gradually fighting its way free of the restrictions placed upon it. On examination, this 'essence' turns out to be heterosexual, and the primary unquestioned heterosexual practice would seem to be that of sexual intercourse. Despite the wealth of work by sociologists and feminists on the social construction of sexuality the idea remains that a natural essence of sexuality exists (Gagnon and Simon, 1973; Jackson, 1978). Another assumption is that there is a unity of interests between men and women in the area of sexuality despite the fact that sexuality represents, above all, a primary area of interaction between two groups of people, men and women, who have very different access to social, economic and political power. Thus, historians who concern themselves with writing the history of the 'regulation of sexuality', without paying serious attention to the way in which the power relationship between the sexes is played out on the field of sexuality, can be seen to be subsuming the interests of women within those of men (Weeks, 1981). A most fundamental assumption is that sexuality is private and personal. It may be understood that social and political pressures influence what happens in the bedroom but sexual behaviour is not recognized as having a dynamic effect in its own right on the structuring of the power relationships in the world which surrounds the bedroom. While sexuality is understood to be the most personal area of private life, it is not surprising that woman's campaigns to set limits to the exercise of male sexuality should be regarded with incomprehension or be totally misunderstood. Ideas and campaigns which are developing within the current wave of feminism give us a very different basis for looking at the work of our foresisters.

Contemporary feminists have detailed the effects upon women of both the fear and the reality of rape, showing that the exercise of male sexuality in the form of rape functions as a form of social control over women's lives (Brownmiller, 1978). Rape as a means of social control has the effect of restricting where women may go, what women may do, serves to 'keep us in our place' which is subordinate to men, and thereby helps to maintain male domination over women. Work is now being done by feminists on the damaging effects upon women caused by the exercise of other aspects of male sexuality. The sexual abuse of children, prostitution, pornography and sexual harassment at work are all now being documented and examined (Barry, 1979; Dworkin, 1981; Lederer, 1981; Mackinnon, 1979; Rush, 1980). Feminists are showing that although these sexual practices by men have consistently been represented as victimless forms of male behaviour, they are in fact crimes against women. Considering that contemporary feminists are having to wage a difficult struggle to get forms of male behaviour which are essentially crimes against women taken seriously, it is not at all surprising that women's campaigns around precisely the same issues in the last wave of feminism are all but invisible to contemporary historians. Much of the feminist theoretical work on male sexual behaviour and its effects on women has been designed to show the ways in which sexual harassment in childhood and in adulthood, at work, on the street and in the home, restricts the lives and opportunities of woman and generally undermines our confidence and self-respect. There has not yet been sufficient work on the collective effect of all the various forms of male sexual behaviour on women's lives so that an estimate can be made of the total importance of male sexual control in the maintenance of women's subordination. However, enough work has been done to indicate that we must look at the area of sexuality, not merely as a sphere of personal fulfilment, but as a battleground; an arena of struggle and power relationships between the sexes.

Current feminist debate on sexuality has gone further than an examination of the effects of male sexuality on women outside the home to a critique of the institution of heterosexuality and its role in the control and exploitation of women. Questions are now being raised about the effects upon women of the experience of sexual activity within all heterosexual relationships in terms of the maintenance of male dominance and female submission (Onlywomen Press, 1981; Rich, 1981). Such questioning allows us to see the feminists engaged in struggles around sexuality in previous generations not simply as the victims of a reactionary ideology, but as women manoeuvring, both to gain more power and control within their own lives, and to remove the restrictions placed upon them by the exercise of male sexuality inside and outside the home.

Social purity

Feminist ideas and personnel played a vitally important part in the development of the 1880s' social purity movement. The most common explanation for the social purity phenomenon given by those historians who have given it any serious attention, is that it was an evangelical, repressive, anti-sex movement (Bristow, 1977). Another approach has been to speak of the anxieties caused by social disruption being displaced on to a concern about sexuality, and to represent the social purity movement as a form of moral panic (Weeks, 1981). Such explanations may help us to understand the involvement of men in social purity. They do not explain the involvement of feminists. Moreover, they do not explain the involvement of women who were not self-consciously feminist or even appear anti-feminist in some of their attitudes. Women share a common experience in relation to the exercise of male sexuality and it is likely that the anxieties which drove them into social purity stemmed from the same source.

Behind the movement of the 1880s lay the agitation around the Contagious Diseases Acts as well as religious 'revivalism'. These Acts in the 1860s allowed compulsory examination of women suspected of working as prostitutes in garrison towns and ports, and the campaign for their repeal gave women the experience of thinking and speaking about previously tabooed topics. Women in the Ladies' National Association inspired by Josephine Butler, were united in indignation against the double standard of sexual morality, men's use of prostitutes and the sexual abuse of children. The feminist opposition to the Acts pointed out that the examinations were an infringement of women's civil rights, and feminists inveighed against the double standard of sexual morality which enforced such abuse of women in order to protect the health of men who, as they pointed out, had infected the prostitutes in the first place. The progenitors of the 1880s' social purity movement were men and women who had been involved in the repeal campaign. The Social Purity Alliance was set up in 1873 by men involved in the campaign to unite those of their sex who wished to transform their conduct and that of other men, so that self-control could be promoted and prostitution rendered unnecessary. From the 1880s onwards and particularly from 1886 when the Contagious Diseases Acts were finally repealed, women who had been involved in the abolition campaign and others who espoused the same principles joined the proliferating social purity organizations in large numbers and brought with them a strong and determined feminist viewpoint. Feminists within the social purity movement fought the assumption that prostitution, which they saw as the sacrifice of women for men, was necessary because of the particular biological nature of male sexuality, and stated that the male sexual urge was a social and not a biological phenomenon. They were particularly outraged at the way in which the exercise of male sexuality created a division of women into the 'pure' and the 'fallen' and prevented the unity of the 'sisterhood of women'. They insisted that men were responsible for prostitution and that the way to end such abuse of women was to curb the demand by enjoining chastity upon men, rather than to punish those who provided the supply. They employed the same arguments in their fight against other aspects of male sexual behaviour which they regarded as damaging to women such as sexual abuse of children, incest, rape and other forms of sexual harassment.

J. Ellice Hopkins's name, unlike that of Josephine Butler, is not generally mentioned in connection with the history of feminism. Her general attitude to the relationship between the sexes owes more to the principles of chivalry than to those of feminism as she reveals in comments such as 'the man is the head of the woman, and is therefore the servant of the woman' (Hopkins, 1882, p. 56). Yet her very considerable contribution to the development of social purity represents in many respects a more militant stance than that of women whose feminist credentials are less ambiguous. An examination of her work throws light on the motivations of all women involved in the social purity campaign; those who had developed feminist consciousness and those who did not. Hopkins described prostitution as the 'degradation of women' and attacked the male use of prostitutes which led to the creation of 'an immense outcast class of helpless women' (Hopkins,

1879, p. 5). In 1879 Hopkins submitted to a committee of convocation 'A plea for the wider action of the Church of England in the prevention of the degradation of women'. The 'plea' was a courageous assault on the hypocrisy of the Church and its indifference to the elimination of prostitution. It was an impassioned demand for action.

Her interest lay, not in punishing women who 'fell', but in protecting women from the damage caused to them by the operation of the double standard and men's sexual practices. She attacked the acceptance by the Church of men's use of women in prostitution in ringing tones:

> the majority of men, many of them good Christian men, hold the necessity of the existence of this outcast class in a civilised country, where marriage is delayed; the necessity of this wholesale sacrifice of women in body and soul (Hopkins, 1879, p. 8).

She demanded that the Church should go further than simply setting up penitentiaries for prostitutes, which merely dealt with the symptoms of the disease, but should aim to cure the disease itself by setting up men's chastity leagues. She carried the battle to protect women from sexual exploitation beyond the defensive activities of preventive and rescue work with women. She directed her energies to the transformation of male sexual behaviour through groups in which men might support each other in exercising self-control.

From Hopkins's efforts emerged the White Cross Army and the Church of England Purity Society, the latter to oversee preventive and rescue work. The purpose of the White Cross Army, formed after a meeting of working men at Edinburgh at which Hopkins spoke, was to circulate literature and enlist the support of men. In 1891 the organizations combined to form the White Cross League which spread to India, Canada, South Africa, the United States, France, Germany, Holland, Switzerland and many more nations. The pledge cards of the White Cross Army show how Hopkins's aim of eliminating the degradation of women was to be fulfilled. The obligations were as follows:

1 To treat all women with respect, and to endeavour to defend them from wrong.
2 To endeavour to put down all indecent language and coarse jests.
3 To maintain the law of purity as equally binding on men and women.

4   To endeavour to spread these principles among my companions and to try to help my younger brothers.
5   To use every possible means to fulfil the command, 'Keep thyself pure' (White Cross League, n.d.).

Hopkins's uncompromising stand on the responsibility of men for the degradation of women was as strong, if not stronger, than that of other feminist campaigners on the issue. In a pamphlet entitled *The Ride of Death* Hopkins describes prostitutes who have 'lost their way' and are close to 'disease, degradation, curses, drink, despair!' She asks:

For who has driven them into that position? Men; men who ought to have protected them, instead of degrading them; men, who have taken advantage of a woman's weakness to gratify their own selfish pleasure, not seeing that a woman's weakness was given to call out a man's strength. Ay, I know that it is often the woman who tempts; these poor creatures must tempt or starve. But that does not touch the broad issue, that it is men who endow the degradation of women; it is men who, making the demand, create the supply. Stop the money of men and the whole thing would be starved out in three months time (Hopkins, n.d., p. 5).

It was common for women involved in the social purity movement to see themselves as being of one accord with what they saw as the women's movement, particularly with respect to work around the area of sexual morality. Hopkins clearly saw herself as part of the women's movement, as she makes clear in this rousing clarion call to other women to join her:

I appeal to you ... not to stand by supinely any longer, and see your own womanhood sunk into degradation, into unnatural uses – crimes against nature, that have no analogue in the animal creation; but, whatever it costs you, to join the vast, silent women's movement which is setting in all over England in defence of your own womanhood .... I appeal to you ... to save the children (Hopkins, 1882, p. 7).

Hopkins did not rely simply on the success of men's chastity leagues in eliminating prostitution and the double standard. Her grand plan for the protection of women and the transformation of male sexual behaviour was to cover the country in a safety net which would include three types of specialized organizations in every town, each with its own tasks to perform. One of these organisations was the Ladies' National

Association for the Care and Protection of Friendless Girls. These associations were set up, after inaugural talks by Hopkins, in towns all over Britain, to establish homes for girls who were homeless, who had come to town looking for work or were between jobs and might otherwise drift into prostitution. The girls were trained in domestic work, fitted with clothing through clothing clubs, and given employment through a free registry office which would not be, as apparently many registry offices were at that time, a front for entrapment into prostitution. By 1879 Ladies' Associations were established in Birmingham, Bristol, Nottingham, London, Edinburgh, Torquay, Cheltenham, Southampton, Winchester, Bedford, Dundee and Perth. During the 1880s they were also formed in many other towns following a visit with a rousing speech and general advice from Ellice Hopkins. Hopkins advised the Ladies' Associations to set up Vigilance Associations in their towns, where these did not already exist, which would concern themselves with indecent printed matter and shows, brother-visiting, and the prosecution of sex offenders. Together the Ladies' Associations, the vigilance societies and the men's chastity leagues represented Hopkins's threefold plan for the elimination of the sexual exploitation of women.

Hopkins's work was fuelled by her anger at the abuse of women implicit is men's use of prostitutes. Her contribution to social purity through her writings and tireless organizing tours was in most respects consonant with the aims of other feminist campaigners on the issue of prostitution. She did, however, encounter criticism for sometimes being less than scrupulous about the civil liberties of women in the actions she took – for example, removing the children of women working as prostitutes to industrial schools. She constantly voiced her support for those who were working to abolish the Contagious Diseases Acts though she chose to put her energies elsewhere. Organizations which emerged as a result of Hopkins's particular vision of the protection of women did not necessarily fulfil her aims. The Church of England Purity Society met with opposition from the staunchly feminist Moral Reform Union over its willingness to support legislation which was restrictive to women.

An issue of major concern to social purity campaigners, particularly the women involved, was the sexual abuse of children. Revelations about the existence of young girls engaged in prostitution emerged from the campaign to repeal the CD Acts and led to the raising of the age of consent for sexual intercourse for girls to 16 in the Criminal Law Amendment Act of 1885. After that Act was passed vigorous agitation continued on the subject of the sexual abuse of children. The organization primarily concerned in this agitation was the National Vigilance Association which was founded directly from the indignation aroused by W. T. Stead's exposure of the 'White Slave Traffic' which involved the buying of young girls for the purpose of prostitution. Women who had been involved in the repeal campaign joined the NVA at its formation in order to continue their work to eliminate the double standard and fight the sexual exploitation of women and girls. The NVA fought not only the sexual abuse of children, but many other forms of sexual harassment of women. The Association or its branches provided solicitors to conduct prosecutions in innumerable cases of rape and attempted rape, sexual assault or indecent exposure, and to take non-judicial action in cases such as the sending of obscene letters to young girls or the sexual harassment of women in the street (NVA, 1886–1905). The NVA sought to implement the terms of the 1885 Act which raised the age of consent and swiftly became concerned about the inadequacies of that legislation for the protection of girls. Much of the energies of the organization went into a campaign to introduce new legislation to remedy the deficiencies of the earlier act. The campaign sought to raise the age of consent for indecent assault (which stayed at 13 in 1885) to 16, to match that for sexual intercourse. It sought to extend the time limit for prosecution which had been fixed at three months in 1885. It also sought to abolish the 'reasonable cause to believe' clause which made it a sufficient defence for a man, charged with defilement of a girl 13 to 16 years old, to prove that he believed she was 16 or older. These clauses, quite exceptional in law, were introduced in the 1885 Act, as NVA women pointed out, specifically to protect the male offenders lest the 1885 Act should be truly effective against them. The NVA also sought to amend the provision in the Act which stipulated that all children's evidence had to be corroborated and which therefore reduced the likelihood of successful prosecution.

After the death penalty for sexual abuse by male family members was abolished during the Restoration, there existed no punishment for such cases in law. NVA members who came across cases of incest were horrified to discover that fathers offending against girls over the age of 16 could not be penalized. They wanted more severe punishment for the abuse of authority and responsibility involved in such cases of incest. The feminist campaigners saw such abuse as an example of the abuse of power. Millicent Fawcett, who ran the Rescue and Preventive sub-committee of the NVA, gave the following explanation for the absence of legislation on incest:

Now this may very probably be a survival of the old evil doctrine of the subjection of women and the absolute supremacy of the head of the family over all members of it .... In all nations of progressive civilisation the history of their progress has consisted in the gradual emancipation of sons, servants, daughters and wives from their former subjection (Fawcett, 1892, p. 3).

She considered that although the emancipation of sons and servants had been accomplished, that of women had not. She said that she was in favour of parental authority but that such authority entailed obligations;

and when a father towards a child, a guardian towards a ward, a master toward a servant, is guilty of using the position of authority the law gives him to induce the child or servant to commit immoral actions, the offence ought to be recognised and punished as having a special degree of gravity (ibid., p. 3).

Like other NVA women, Fawcett wanted to enshrine in law the principle that men who abused a position of trust and advantage by exploiting young girls should receive harsher sentences. It was proposed that incest legislation should be included in an act covering abuse by guardians, employers, schoolmasters, and managers of amusement arcades. The Punishment of Incest Act, which was finally achieved in 1908, did not fulfil these broad aims. The raising of the age of consent for indecent assault to 16 was only achieved in 1922 after a concerted campaign by a wide range of women's organizations.

The fight for legislative reform was not the only method adopted by feminists in their determination to protect children from sexual exploitation and to support the victims. There were also campaigns for women police to work with the women and girls involved in sex offence cases; to ensure that women doctors would examine abused children, and that women magistrates would deal with cases; to establish playgrounds in parks to which adult males would be denied access and women-only carriages in trains for the protection of women and girls. Women also campaigned to educate public opinion on the subject, particularly around the issue of the male bias of judges and juries. The suffrage journals, women in the NVA and other organizations and

Lady Astor in the House of Commons (after she became the first woman MP) all monitored the sentencing of offenders against children, and found that judges not only gave lenient sentences, but were prepared to accuse victims as young as 7 years old of being seductive. One judge excused an offender on the grounds that 'this was the sort of thing which might happen to any man' (Conference on Criminal Assaults on Children, 1914). Some women formed themselves into 'watch' committees to monitor each case in their area that came before the courts, in order to show that the magistrates were under surveillance and that their sentencing policy would be publicized (*Assaults on Children*, 1914). These examples give only a taste of the vast quantity of activity being carried out by women around the issue of sexual abuse.

From the beginning there was a current of opinion within the social purity movement which ran strictly counter to that of the feminist campaigners. Some men and women within the movement were prepared to sacrifice women in the cause of eliminating prostitution by promoting legislation which restricted or penalized prostitutes and yet failed to punish the men who used them. The feminists vigorously opposed such ideas and practices wherever they appeared. One strongly feminist organization, the Moral Reform Union (1881–97) wrote to and attended meetings of those societies which it saw as promoting unjust legislation, and demanded that they take the views of women into account. These societies included the Central Vigilance Committee and the Church of England Purity Society (Moral Reform Union, 1883, p. 6; 1884, p. 13).

In the late nineteenth and early twentieth centuries many feminists changed their tactics and concentrated on the suffrage campaign in the hope that the vote would provide a solution to the problem of the sexual abuse of women and girls. They hoped that legislation introduced through the new women's vote and by women MPs would strengthen the law on sex offences and help improve women's wages so that the poverty which drove women into prostitution would not be so acute. Other feminists despaired of the attitudes of those social purity campaigners who were attacking 'vice' itself rather than the abuse of women and felt unable to work with them. As feminist energies were withdrawn, many social purity organizations fell under the domination of these anti-vice crusaders.

Feminist ideas on sexuality: Elizabeth Wollstenholme Elmy and Frances Swiney

Two feminists, Elizabeth Wollstenholme Elmy and Frances Swiney, who were heavily involved in the suffrage campaign as well as other feminist issues, wrote extensively on sexuality and their writings give us an insight into the ideas and motivations which lay behind feminist agitation on the subject. Both were greatly concerned with prostitution and the sexual abuse of children, but they went further than other women involved in the campaigns by asserting a woman's right to control her own body within marriage and by developing a theoretical analysis of the sexual oppression of women.

In a feminist career which spanned sixty years, Elizabeth Wollstenholme Elmy worked alongside the women who were taking the most radical stand on sexuality, such as Josephine Butler and Christabel Pankhurst. Her main campaigning activities were in the areas of higher education for women, women's suffrage, reform of the laws on marriage and custody, and the abolition of the Contagious Diseases Acts. She generally wrote under the pseudonym 'Ellis Ethelmer'. Of her major works, two are books on sex education for children: one, *Woman Free*, is a heavily annotated poem mainly concerned with women's biology and the effects of sexual abuse; and another, *Phases of Love*, is concerned with the ideal form of the sex relation between men and women. Many of her articles pursue the same themes. Her activities in the Ladies' National Association and in marriage reform gave her practical outlets for her views. Most of her writings date from the 1890s.

Frances Swiney began writing in the 1890s and published a great quantity of books, pamphlets and articles up to the First World War. Her ideas were clearly influential in the women's movement and her books were reviewed and advertised in *The Suffragette* (edited by Christabel Pankhurst) and other suffrage journals. A friendship developed between Swiney and Wollstenholme Elmy out of their activities in the suffrage campaign. Both saw the sexual subjection of women as fundamental to the oppression of women by men. They offered similar solutions which involved the elimination of physical sexual activity between men and women as far as possible and the promotion of sexual self-control for men. Wollstenholme Elmy's solution was psychic love; Swiney's was her own particular brand of theosophy promoted through the League of Isis which she organized. Wollstenholme Elmy showed no reluctance in stating the facts of sexual life, and went so far as to write clear and simple descriptions of the human reproductive process for children at a time when many considered ignorance to be a virtue in adult women, let alone in children. The book for older children, published in 1892, was entitled *The Human Flower*. It begins with a description of reproduction in flowers and goes on to describe human reproduction in a manner designed, as she said, to prevent any stigma of 'impurity' from being attached to any part of the human body. In pursuit of this aim the human genitals are described as 'flower-like' organs. The book for younger children was entitled, appropriately, *Baby Buds*.

The central theme of Wollstenholme Elmy's writings was the right of women to control their own bodies. This control was to extend to decisions of when and how sexual activity should take place and whether or not to have children. In her sex education book for teenagers she writes of the horror of sexual coercion of the wife by the husband, presumably so that the idea of mutuality and the woman's right to decide should be implanted at an early age. In *The Human Flower* she laments the ignorance of most women entering marriage of the 'marital intimacies, which, unless of reciprocal impulse, may prove repugnant and intolerable to her' (Ethelmer, 1892, p. 43). Wollstenholme Elmy left her young readers in no doubt as to the importance of woman's control of her own body:

the conviction is every day growing that under no plea or promise can it be permissible to submit the individuality, either mental or physical, of the wife, to the will and coercion of the husband; the functions of wifehood and motherhood must remain solely and entirely within the wife's own option. Coercion, like excess, is in itself a contravention and annihilation of the psychic nature of the sexual relation; since no true affection or love would either prompt or permit to inflict a grief or an injustice on a reluctant partner, and to submit her thus to the possibility of undesired maternity is a procedure equally unjustifiable and inhuman to the mother and the 'unwelcome child' (Ethelmer, 1892, p. 43).

She carried her indignation at sexual coercion in marriage further by campaigning to get the right of women to refuse sexual intercourse in marriage recognized in law. From 1880 onwards, when a Criminal

Code Bill was drawn up which embodied in statute law the fact that a man could not be accused of raping his wife, women sought to show that such an enactment would reduce the wife to 'bodily slavery'. The women's campaign was unsuccessful: a hundred years later it is still not an offence for a husband to rape his wife.

Although Wollstenholme Elmy was in favour of eliminating sexual intercourse other than for the purposes of reproduction, in her sex education literature she merely pointed out the necessity for strict mutuality, combined with the hint that some couples chose only to engage in sexual intercourse for procreation, which obviated the need for birth control. *Phases of Love* (Ethelmer, 1897) is far more explicit. The book is described as 'A history of the human passion and of its advance from the physical to the psychic character and attribute'. Her main idea is that the history of the human race is a story of the transformation of physical into psychic love. She writes of previous and less enlightened historical systems that 'into each of these masculine schemes was interwoven, with a singular unanimity, the bodily subjection (and hence the degradation) of women' (Ethelmer, 1897, p. 9). She describes how throughout history men had misused women by 'positive physical oppression and excess' which had resulted in a restriction of woman's 'native individuality of mental power and action' (ibid., p. 23). Her anger at the way that woman was reduced by men's obsession with physical sex love to a merely sexual function, is echoed again and again through the development of feminist thought from the mid nineteenth century through to the 1920s. Wollstenholme Elmy's solution was to promote the ideal of sexual self-control and its counterpart of 'psychic love', which from her description does not seem to have been devoid of physical satisfactions as well as emotional ones. Her aim was to free woman from the 'degradation of her bodily temple to solely animal uses' (ibid., p. 46) so that she might take a full part in all the areas of life previously arrogated to man.

Wollstenholme Elmy is most remembered and quoted by historians not for her outspoken attacks on sexual coercion in marriage, or her brave accounts of human reproduction for children, but for saying that menstruation was pathological and caused by men's sexual abuse of women – an idea that she did not invent but took straight from the work of contemporary male doctors (Maclaren, 1978, p. 198). Similarly, the treatment of Frances Swiney by historians has tended to be cursory or dismissive, interpreting her work as that of either a crank or a prude (Mitchell, 1977, p. 319).

Swiney was a passionate feminist who described in great detail the nature of female oppression and the way in which women were kept in an inferior position. At the root of women's wrongs she placed the sexual subjection of women, and it is on this that she concentrates in her writings. She was a matriarchalist and believed that the oppression of women began when men destroyed the matriarchate to make women into sexual slaves who would satisfy their sexual desires. Like Wollstenholme Elmy she accused men of having reduced women to a purely sexual function:

Men have sought in women only a body. They have possessed that body. They have made it the refuse heap of sexual pathology, when they should have reverenced it as the Temple of God, The Holy Fane of Life, the Fountain of Health to the human race (Swiney, 1907, p. 43).

The greatest burden of this sexual subjection was that women were forced to submit to sexual intercourse whenever the male desired, and even at those times which Swiney believed should be most sacred, during pregnancy and immediately after childbirth. She considered such use of the woman's body to be abusive, and employed quantities of biological, medical and anthropological evidence to prove her point. She was angry at the subjection of women to unwanted childbearing and her indignation was stimulated by the gynaecological discoveries which were being revealed in the medical literature of the time. It seemed to Swiney that the constant ailments suffered by the nineteenth-century women stemmed largely from a practice which was imposed by man upon woman and which was quite unnecessary save for procreation, that of sexual intercourse. She listed the effects of venereal diseases which were just coming to light and the many vaginal infections and ailments of the reproductive system which women suffered as a result of sexual intercourse. Some of these sound far-fetched. Many are simply the facts with which women's health handbooks concern themselves today. One of her revelations, now supported by current medical opinion, was that of the link between sperm and cervical cancer. The following quotation demonstrates the power of her rhetoric and the vehemence of her indictment of man:

Church and State, religion, law, prejudice, custom, tradition, greed, lust, hatred, injustice, selfishness, ignorance, and arrogance have all conspired against her under the sexual rule of the human male. Vices, however, like curses, come back to roost. In his own enfeebled frame, in his diseased tissues, in his weak will, his gibbering idiocy, his raving insanity, and hideous criminality, he reaps the fruits of a dishonoured motherhood, an outraged womanhood, an unnatural, abnormal, stimulated childbirth, and a starved poison-fed infancy .... (Swiney, 1907, p. 38).

Swiney's solution to the problem of women being seen purely as the objects of men's sexual use, as well as to the contradictions of sexual intercourse in the forms of unwanted pregnancy and disease, was the 'Law of Continence' or 'Natural Law'. She asserted that sexual intercourse should take place only for the purpose of reproduction and never on any account during periods of lactation or gestation. According to her plan, which included very extended periods of lactation, a woman could be expected to bear children at intervals of four to five years. To support her argument she referred to the work of contemporary anthropologists who described societies in which women had no more than three or four children and would not allow men sexual access to them for periods of from two to twelve years.

Swiney codified the 'Natural Law' into a religious system for the theosophical society she administered, the League of Isis. The six rules of observance of the society all concerned the regulation of sexual activity according to the 'Natural Law'. Through continence, and only continence, the spiritual aims of theosophists could be realized by the transmutation of physical into mental energy. Such a religious system must have been of positive advantage to women who wished to avoid sexual intercourse, since they could point out that the unwanted activity could be damaging to the 'higher self'. It seems likely that the great appeal of theosophy to women in the late nineteenth and early twentieth centuries lay in the justification it gave to continence in men and 'psychic love' for women. The most famous convert to theosophy and perhaps the most dramatic, since she went from being an advocate and practitioner of free love to being a most energetic proponent of celibacy – to the astonishment and discomfiture of her friends – was Annie Besant (Besant, 1877–1901). Christian social purity, celibate theosophy and the 'psychic love' of a freethinker like Wollstenholme Elmy all contained the advantage that they promoted and justified sexual self-control in men.

Sexuality and the suffrage 1906–14

The struggle in the area of sexuality gained momentum in the period of suffrage activity before the First World War. The whole range of suffrage organizations – the Conservative and Unionist Women's Franchise Association, the Women's Freedom League, the Men's League for Women's Suffrage, the National Union of Women's Suffrage Societies, the Church League for Women's Suffrage, and the Women's Social and Political Union – issued statements on the double standard and on prostitution which were practically identical in tone. In this intense phase of the suffrage struggle, the vote was presented as a cure-all for women's grievances. Suffragists of all persuasions proclaimed that when women had the vote they would enforce chastity on men and end the abuse of women in prostitution, the sale of women in the 'White Slave' traffic, and the sexual abuse of children. The suffragists were involved in a crusade to transform male sexuality and the WSPU was at the forefront. Lucy Re-Bartlett, an admirer of the WSPU, wrote that few realized the 'underlying situation' behind the great struggle for women's suffrage, and its 'magnitude and inevitability':

The public roughly seems to be divided between people who deny to the struggle any sexual significance at all, and those who, seeing this significance, attribute it to sexual morbidity and hysteria, while the truth, in fact, lies in neither of these extremes (Re-Bartlett, 1912, p. 28).

Re-Bartlett suggests that the struggle actually signified the transition of men and women from 'spiritual childhood' to 'spiritual adulthood'.

A new focus for the feminist struggle around sexuality at this stage was provided by the issue of venereal disease. Christabel Pankhurst took up this issue as a tactical move. In an article written in 1913, 'The Suffragette', she explained that raising the issue of sexual vice was a final massive effort to inspire women with the anger and energy which would gain success in the suffrage struggle. She wrote, 'We have here the thing which will appeal to and unite all women' (22 April). She was writing at a time when there was considerable public concern about the prevalence of venereal disease and medical research was at last demonstrating the real and alarming physical effects of the diseases as well as producing the first really effective cures. There was much information at her disposal. In *The Great Scourge and How to End It*

(1913) she detailed the effects of venereal disease, pointing out how the diseases affected the wives and children of infected men. She claimed that 75 to 80 per cent of men had gonorrhoea and a considerable proportion of the rest had syphilis. The solution was 'Votes for Women: and chastity for men' (Pankhurst, 1913, p. 3). The pamphlet contains a lengthy description of what she considered to be wrong with male sexuality.

The serious critique of male sexuality which was launched by feminists in this period continued to be based on the idea that woman was maintained in 'sex-slavery' by being seen in terms of sex and no other function. Christabel Pankhurst wrote that sexual disease was due to the 'doctrine that woman is sex and beyond that nothing', and that the result of the untrammelled expression of male sexual desires was that the 'relationship between man and woman has centred in the physical' and that the relationship had become that of 'master and slave' (ibid, p. 20). This idea was echoed by Cicely Hamilton in her book *Marriage as a Trade* (1909/1981) and by contributors to the debate on sexuality in *The Freewoman* magazine in 1911 and 1912.

The sexualization of women was supported by the idea, common to sex reformers and anti-feminists of the period, that the male sexual urge was enormously powerful, almost insatiable and difficult if not impossible to control. The feminists argued, as they had been doing since the women's movement began, that the male urge was constructed and was not a natural endowment of man. It could therefore be retrained and transformed. This refutation of the naturalness of men's sexual abuse of women was potentially revolutionary in its implications for the relations between the sexes. Frances Swiney had scorned the 'large majority of persons, ignorant of physiology (who) still believe in the exploded fallacy of man's necessity for physical sexual expression and the need for its gratification' (Swiney, n.d., p. 38). She wrote that 'Woman's redemption from sex-slavery can only be achieved through man's redemption from sex-obsession' (ibid., p. 38). Christabel Pankhurst devoted a chapter in *The Great Scourge* to quashing the argument that sexual intercourse was necessary to men's health and quoted fifteen doctors who maintained that continence was not harmful to men and did not cause the genital organs to atrophy. Emmeline Pankhurst joined in the debate as fiercely as her daughter. Commenting on a speech by a man who said that there would always be prostitution she wrote:

If it is true – I do not believe it for one moment – that men have less power of self control than women have, or might have if properly educated, if there is a terrible distinction between the physical and moral standards of both sexes, then I say as a woman, representing thousands of women all over the world, men must find some way of supplying the needs of their sex which does not include the degradataion of ours (*The Suffragette*, 29 August 1913).

Many other aspects of men's sexual behaviour came in for criticism by feminists, such as a lack of 'sympathy and gentleness' and the practice of separating sexual activity from the context of emotional relationships.

Judging by their own statements, the reaction of anti-feminist writers and the furore about them in the press, some feminists were choosing, before the First World War, not to have any sexual relations with men. No longer content merely with a critique of male sexual behaviour and a campaign to promote chastity for men, these women were proclaiming the virtue of remaining unmarried and celibate. They were taking this decision to protest against the form taken by male sexuality and the way in which women were oppressed in relationships with men, and because some of them believed that the position of all women could only be improved in a society where there was a large class of celibate women. It is difficult to judge the size of this revolt or precisely what it meant to all the women involved, but the amount of anxiety it created among anti-feminists and even some feminists suggests that it is worth serious examination. The sex imbalance in the population reached a peak in the 1901 census with 1068 women to every 1000 men and it remained at this level in the 1911 census. This imbalance provided a material basis for the alarm of anti-feminists at 'surplus women' and suggested to some of the feminist proponents of celibacy that nature was on their side. More importantly, the rate of marriage was low in the pre-war period. 1911 represents a peak in the number of women who remained single in each age group from 25 upwards. The proportion of women to men in the population rose in the 1921 census but the rate of marriage in every age group also rose after the war. Though 1911 does not represent the all time high in the proportion of women to men it does seem to have represented an all time low in the popularity of marriage.

Christabel Pankhurst stated categorically that spinsterhood was a political decision, a deliberate choice made in response to the conditions of sex-slavery:

There can be no mating between the spiritually developed women of this new day and men who in thought and conduct with regard to sex matters are their inferiors (Pankhurst, 1913, p. 98).

It can reasonably be assumed that she was not alone in her views in the WSPU, since in the same year (1913) 63 per cent of members were spinsters and many of the rest were widows.

Cicely Hamilton's book *Marriage as a Trade* (1909) is a lengthy exposition of why women wished to be spinsters, the ploys used against them and her belief in the political necessity of spinsters to the women's revolution. The importance of spinsters was that only they could help advance the cause of women as 'any improvement as has already been effected in the status of the wife and mother has originated outside herself, and is, to a great extent, the work of the formerly contented spinster' (Hamilton, 1909, p. 252). As the spinster improved her position she steadily destroyed the prestige of marriage, and the conditions of marriage would have to be improved if there was seen to be a viable alternative to marriage open to women. If marriage was voluntary and not enforced, she thought, men would have to pay for the work they then got for nothing and would have to exercise self-control instead of seeing 'one half of the race as sent into the world to excite desire in the other half (Hamilton, 1909, p. 278).

Lucy Re-Bartlett, in the course of her eulogy to the militant suffragettes, proclaimed that the phenomenon of celibacy among feminists and other women was a positive decision to refuse to enter into relationships with men until the animal nature of men was transformed and a new spiritual form of relationship between the sexes was possible. In *Sex and Sanctity*, after speaking of the 'horrors of the White Slave Traffic' and the 'ruin of little children', she describes the 'new social conscience' arising in Britain and in other countries. These women, she declared:

feel linked by their womanhood to every suffering woman, and every injured child, and as they look around upon the great mass of men who seem to them indifferent, there is growing up in the hearts of some of these women a great sense of distance .... In the hearts of many women today is rising a cry somewhat like this: ... I will know no man, and bear no child until this apathy is broken through – these wrongs be righted (Re-Bartlett, 1912, p. 125).

She wrote that both married and single women were feeling and acting thus: 'It is the "silent strike" and it is going on all over the world' (ibid., p. 44).

The development of a class of spinsters proud to proclaim that they were happy, fulfilled, had made a deliberate choice and were vital to the political struggle of women, met with serious opposition. From the 1890s onwards there had been developing from the work of Edward Carpenter, Havelock Ellis and their circle, and the publication of *The Adult* magazine, a body of sex-reforming ideas. These ideas, particularly those concerning the physical necessity of sexual intercourse to both sexes and the dangers of 'repression', were represented in the women's movement before the First World War and were used to launch a savage propaganda battle against the 'spinster'. *The Freewoman* magazine gave the opposition its platform. The magazine was founded in 1911 by Dora Marsden, who had previously been involved in militant suffrage activity. It was dedicated to promoting the ideas of the sex reformers and carried articles on removing restrictions on women's freedom to relate sexually to men, marriage law reform, the promotion of unmarried love and criticisms of monogamy. The spinster-baiting in *The Freewoman* was conducted alongside a protracted propaganda campaign against the WSPU. The assault on spinsters started in the very first issue. In an article entitled 'The Spinster' written 'by one', the class of 'unhusbanded women' is given a destructive and twisted character. The opening lines indicate the general tone.

I write of the High Priestess of Society. Not of the mother of sons, but of her barren sister, the withered tree, the acidulous vestal under whose pale shadow we chill and whiten, of the Spinster I write. Because of her power and dominion. She, unobtrusive, meek, soft-footed, silent, shamefaced, bloodless and boneless, thinned to spirit, enters the secret recesses of the mind, sits at the secret springs of action, and moulds and fashions our emasculate society. She is our social nemesis (*The Freewoman*, 23 November 1911).

In subsequent issues of *The Freewoman* further articles appeared purporting to describe how various varieties of spinsters emerged. One on the college-educated woman spoke in disapproving tones of her growing lack of interest in clothes, lack of sex attraction and indifference to men. Central to the first article was the argument common to the works of the sex-reforming fraternity, that sexual activity with men was vital to the health of women and that without it they became either bitter and twisted or gushingly sentimental. A debate then ensued in the letters pages of the magazine in which the spinsters sought to defend their position. They argued that it was in fact marriage which was ruinous to the health of women and that they were, as spinsters, perfectly happy and healthy. They also argued for the political necessity of a class of spinsters. A correspondence developed between Kathryn Oliver, a spinster, and 'New Subscriber' who subsequently identified herself as Stella Browne. Oliver attacked the 'new morality' saying that she was an 'apostle of the policy of self-restraint in sex-matters' (15 February 1912). She denied that celibacy endangered women's health. Stella Browne assured readers that many women's health, happiness, social usefulness and mental capacity were 'seriously impaired sometimes totally ruined by the unnatural conditions of their lives', if they were celibate. She proclaimed that 'sex is a Joy' and bewailed the effects of such women as Oliver on the women's movement:

It will be an unspeakable catastrophe if our richly complex Feminist movement with its possibilities of power and joy, falls under the domination of sexually deficient and disappointed women, impervious to facts and logic and deeply ignorant of life (7 March 1912).

There is no doubt that Stella Browne and other sex-reforming feminists after her, such as Dora Russell, were passionately interested in promoting women's right to sexual pleasure as a vital component of the struggle for women's emancipation. In order to promote the joy of sex they found it necessary to be uncompromising in their attack on all those whom they considered to be standing in the way of this march to sexual freedom including, just before the First World War, the vast majority of feminists and particularly the spinsters within their ranks. In the period immediately before the war the women's movement was deeply divided over the issue of sexuality. One camp advocated the joys and necessities of heterosexual intercourse, in or out of marriage, without any serious attempt to criticize the form of male sexuality and its effects on women, presumably because such criticism would have detracted from the strength of their campaign. The other camp pointed out that many women received no joy from sexual intercourse, suggested that there were large differences of interest between men and women over the issue of sexuality, launched a major critique of the form of male sexuality and advocated non-cooperation with the sexual desires of men.

The vast majority of feminist campaigners in the 'first wave' of feminism challenged the form taken by male sexuality and sought to transform and set limits to male sexual behaviour in order to protect women from the damaging effects of rape and sexual assault, prostitution and the sexual abuse of children, sexual coercion in marriage and unwanted childbearing. Some saw the 'sex-slavery' which reduced women to a purely sexual function and restricted their lives and opportunities as fundamental to the oppression of women. The tactics they employed included the setting up of men's chastity leagues, supporting the victims, campaigns of propaganda to enlighten public opinion, the development of spiritual systems, a concentration on the struggle for the vote as a cure-all and total withdrawal from sexual relations with men. The sheer volume of activities engaged in by feminists and the strength of the anger and sense of outrage they expressed suggest that these campaigns were a dominant theme of the women's movement and a very strong motivation behind it.

After the First World War and particularly after the passing of the 1922 Act which raised the age of consent for indecent assault to 16, this aspect of the women's movement suffered rapid decline. This decline was concurrent with a general decline of militant feminism and with the triumph of 'sex reform' in the 1920s. The 1920s witnessed a concerted campaign through marriage advice literature and clinics, as well as the works of 'progressive' and conservative sex reformers, to conscript women into participation in sexual intercourse with men, combined with a sustained assault by the sex reformers on 'the spinster', the 'frigid' women, militant feminists, 'man-haters' and, in particular, women campaigners who were launching a critique of male sexuality. The connection between the decline of militant feminism and the development of the sex reform movement is one of the most interesting questions to emerge from an examination of the literature on sexuality of the 1920s, and it forms the subject of my continuing research.

2 Sexology and the social construction of male sexuality (Havelock Ellis)*

Margaret Jackson

This chapter represents a small part of a much larger project in progress on the relationship between women's liberation and sexual liberation. The project is focused primarily on the period 1914–39, when feminism, relative to the pre-First World War years, became de-radicalized and suffered a decline. There is some evidence to suggest a relationship between the decline of feminism and the development of an ideology of sexual liberation. There is also a clear connection between the development of the ideology of sexual liberation and the development of sexology throughout the twentieth century, and especially in the first three decades. A key figure in the new 'science' of sex at this time was Havelock Ellis, and this chapter is chiefly a critique of his ideas. My aim is to raise questions about the social construction of sexuality, especially male sexuality and heterosexual relations, as well as the concepts of sexual 'desire' and 'pleasure', particularly female sexual pleasure. I do so in the belief that it is crucial for feminists to understand the historical process of such constructions if we are to develop effective strategies for changing the social relations of the sexes.

The basic assumption on which my work rests is that sexuality does not merely reflect but is fundamental to the construction and maintenance of power relations between women and men. This is not to deny either the importance of other dimensions of the social relations of the sexes, or the complex relationships between women's oppression and other oppressions, particularly race and class. I have concentrated on sexuality partly because it is an area which has been relatively

*This chapter was first published in *Women's Studies International Forum*, **6** no. 1 (1983)

neglected at the theoretical level (in contrast to other areas, such as domestic labour, women and the state, etc.), but mainly because what is *specific* to the oppression of women of all races and classes is that it takes a *sexual* form. Women constitute the only oppressed class which is dominated and controlled through sexuality, both directly, by means of rape and other forms of overt sexual coercion, and indirectly, by being taught to experience the sexual colonization of our bodies as sexual pleasure.[1]

Sexual liberation or women's liberation?

It is the latter aspect of the socio-sexual control of women by men which primarily concerns me here. The concept of sexual pleasure – together with the whole cluster of related concepts such as sex drive, sexual desire, sexual repression etc. – has for too long been taken for granted, both by sexual 'radicals', who wrongly equate sexual liberation with women's liberation, and by those (including some feminists) who have attempted a critical analysis of sexual ideologies and practices.[2] Both share the assumption, common among all who might be loosely termed 'progressive' in matters of sex, that sexual pleasure is A Good Thing, which everyone should have an equal right to, male or female, gay or straight. What form the sexual pleasure takes is considered to be a matter of personal choice – a curiously individualistic stance, given that most sexual radicals are also socialists; and it is strongly implied, and sometimes explicitly stated, that one has no right to criticize sexual 'minorities' such as paedophiles and sado-masochists, for their particular sexual preference.[3]

In what follows I hope to show that the implications of this ideology of sexual liberation are profoundly anti-feminist, and that the main reason for this lies in the failure to make problematic the concept of sexual pleasure. What counts as sexual pleasure, who defines it, who has the power to ensure that certain definitions prevail? Unless we explore these and many other related questions we may find ourselves in the position of asserting a 'right' to something that is not in our interests as women struggling to end male supremacy. One way of examining the concept of sexual pleasure, and the broader conceptions of sexuality in which it is embedded, is to look at their development historically, and at the relationship between ideas about sex and the socio-political context in which they take root.

Sexology: the social construction of sexual knowledge

Our notions of sexual pleasure have been shaped by many factors, but one of the most important twentieth-century influences has been sexology – the 'science' of sex. Its importance lies in the fact that, as a science, it enjoys tremendous status and legitimacy, science being the twentieth-century god. The findings of the sexologists, from Havelock Ellis through Kinsey to Masters and Johnson, have found their way into sex education, marriage manuals, counselling and sex therapy, as well as 'common sense' notions about sex. Most liberals, socialists and many feminists have viewed the influence of sexology as progressive, in promoting healthier attitudes to sex and thus contributing to sexual liberation, and, by a false extension, women's liberation. In particular, the work of the early twentieth-century pioneers of sexology has been seen as leading everyone out of the 'darkness' of Victorian prudery and sexual repression into the 'light' of twentieth-century sexual freedom.

Havelock Ellis has been especially applauded as one of the first to champion a woman's right to sexual pleasure. He himself, indeed, claimed to be asserting the 'erotic rights' of women on their behalf (Ellis, 1918). This alone would seem to indicate the need for a feminist appraisal of his ideas. Furthermore, it is generally acknowledged that Ellis did more than anyone in the English-speaking world to establish sexology as a science; and that his influence on modern conceptions of sexuality has been enormous – as great, in some respects, as Freud's. It seems to me, then, that if as feminists we are to understand how our sexuality, and our thinking about sexuality, have been shaped historically, an examination of Ellis's ideas and influence is absolutely crucial.

Havelock Ellis: sexologist and ideologist

Ellis's historical significance as a producer of sexual knowledge is widely recognized. He is generally regarded as not merely a pioneer sexologist but a torchbearer of sexual enlightenment, a trail-blazer of the sexual revolution. Robinson (1976) sees him as one of the most influential sexual thinkers of this century after Freud; and together with Freud, Kinsey and Masters and Johnson, one of those most responsible for the way we have come to conceive of our sexuality. He has assessed him as the central figure in the emergence of the modern sexual ethos, standing in the same relation to modern sexual theory as Albert Einstein to modern physics. Brecher (1970), who claimed to be the first historian of sex research, dubbed Ellis 'the first of the yea-sayers', who inaugurated the gradual convalescence of our culture from a debilitating sexual disease, i.e. sexual puritanism, but whose commitment to sex reform did not impair his objectivity as a scientist; he saw him as essentially a naturalist, observing rather than judging. Ellis's most recent biographer views him as a revolutionary, 'one of the seminal figures responsible for the creation of a modern sensibility', who punctured the prejudices and misconceptions of the Victorian view of sex (Grosskurth, 1980, p. 15).

The two particular features of Ellis's work which have contributed most to his popularity, especially with sexual radicals, are 1   his recognition of the existence of female sexuality and the importance of sexual pleasure for both sexes, and 2   his broadening of the range of legitimate sexual behaviour, which helped to promote greater tolerance of sexual deviance, particularly homosexuality. Sheila Rowbotham, for example, has argued that Stella Browne's sexual radicalism owed much to Ellis, and refers to having been told how people sat round reading Ellis in a Communist Party branch in the 1930s, implying that they considered this terribly progressive (Rowbotham, 1977). Weeks (1977) has examined Ellis's contribution to the liberalizing of attitudes towards homosexuality and, more generally, to the formulation of liberal sexual ideology (Rowbotham and Weeks, 1977; Weeks, 1981). He has described him as 'ultimately, a cautious sex reformer rather than a sexual radical', though he sees this as heightening rather than diminishing his importance (Weeks, 1981, p. 152). He points out his failure to challenge stereotypes of masculinity and femininity, in relation both to sexuality and to the respective social roles of men and women, and notes his inadequate treatment of lesbianism. Weeks also draws attention to the apparent paradox that Ellis on the one hand 'recognised the necessity of women controlling their own sexuality' while, on the other, argued that nature defined woman's true sphere as motherhood (Rowbotham and Weeks, 1977, p. 178). Thus, while advocating contraception and abortion, he was strongly opposed to women's employment outside the home and to the idea of nursery provision. He firmly believed that every healthy woman ought to exercise her reproductive function at least once in her lifetime, and asserted that women's brains were 'in a certain sense ... in their wombs'

(Ellis, 1913, vol. 3, p. 253). Although he claimed to be pro-feminist, he was extremely hostile to militant feminism, and particularly to the Women's Social and Political Union (led by the Pankhursts).

Weeks implies that Ellis's reactionary views on woman's role stemmed partly from a failure to appreciate a socialist analysis of the relationship between capitalism and the position of women, and partly from the fact that he was trapped within stereotyped images that he had inherited. It seems to me, however, that Weeks sees a paradox where none exists; and that he sees it because he is blinkered by the ideology of sexual liberation. In common with most other 'critics' of Ellis, he has failed to question the assumption that sexual liberation implies women's liberation, and to situate Ellis's work adequately in its socio-political context; thus he describes the leaders of the Women's Movement as 'conservative', because they shunned Ellis's support (allegedly in case his reputation damaged their cause). Recent feminist work, however, suggests on the contrary a negative association between sex reform and women's liberation. It suggests that the politics of sex reform and feminist sexual politics were, in Ellis's time – as they are still – in many respects mutually antagonistic, and that the feminist opposition to sexual 'liberation', far from being simplistically conservative, reflected a conviction that it was not in women's interests.

Feminism and sexology: sex and social control

The development of sexology in the late nineteenth and early twentieth centuries must be seen in the context of changes in the social and economic position of women and the feminist challenge to male supremacy. Sexology is, after all, about *sex*, and the specifically sexual exploitation and oppression of women by men has always been a central strand of feminism. The demand of the Women's Movement of the late nineteenth and early twentieth centuries was *not* for 'a woman's right to sexual pleasure', though certain individual feminists, such as Stella Browne, Emma Goldman, Ellen Key and others, did proclaim the joys of (heterosexual) sex, frequently coupled with fulfilment through motherhood. The demand of the Women's Movement, in Britain and America, from the mid nineteenth century right up to the First World War (and beyond), was for female sexual autonomy; a demand that was seen as inseparable from the necessity of bringing male sexuality under control. As Elizabeth Cady Stanton wrote, in a letter to Susan Anthony in 1853: 'man in his lust has regulated this whole question of sexual intercourse long enough' (Sinclair, 1966, p. 72). This demand was generally known as the demand for an equal moral standard, and was, at the height of the militant suffrage campaign, succinctly conveyed by the slogan: 'Votes for Women, Chastity for Men'. It has been dismissed by some as a demand for equal sexual repression, an interpretation which owes much to liberal, and especially post-Freudian, sexual ideology.[4]

Sheila Jeffreys' account of the feminist campaigns around sexuality up to the First World War (see Chapter 1) has shown that women's campaigns around prostitution, venereal disease, the sexual abuse of children, rape in marriage etc., represented an attack on male ownership and control of women's bodies, which was seen as central to women's subordination. Women such as Josephine Butler, Elizabeth Wollstenholme Elmy, Jane Ellice Hopkins, Frances Swiney, and later Cicely Hamilton and Christabel Pankhurst, challenged the myth that the sexual abuse and exploitation of women and girls was an unfortunate but inevitable result of men's natural sexual urges. They clearly saw male sexuality as a consequence of male power, not male biology, and they demanded that men exercise sexual self-control. They were not prudes, or against sex *per se*, and some were apparently not against marriage as such; but they argued that frequent sexual intercourse was neither necessary nor desirable, and was often positively harmful. Most feminists before the First World War were extremely wary of artificial contraception, believing that it would increase the level of sexual exploitation of women; instead they advocated abstinence as a means of birth control. Many feminists refused to marry or to have sexual relationships with men, and the pre-First World War period saw a significant increase in the number of spinsters, the rate of marriage falling to a record low level in 1911. Some explicitly advocated sexual withdrawal from men as a political strategy.[5]

My argument is that it is against this background, as well as the beginnings of a more general erosion of male supremacy at the turn of the century, that the development of sexology, and especially the new doctrine of sexual pleasure, must be seen. I suggest that Ellis's work in particular can be interpreted as part of a response, however unconscious, to the threat to male power posed by the feminist onslaught on male sexuality. There is already a considerable body of feminist analysis which seems to point in this direction. Linda Gordon, for example, has shown how in the early twentieth century the American medical profession, influenced by European sex theorists, began to support the idea of birth control by arguing against continence, and acclaimed free sexual 'expression' as leading to liberation. 'Self-control' was now asserted to be debilitating and damaging, and the single standard of morality demanded by feminists pronounced as 'impractical'. Feminists were pilloried as sexually frustrated women who got that way by denying their true destinies. Many of them, however, continued to insist that 'sexual freedom' was neither liberating nor progressive but reactionary. Charlotte Perkins Gilman, for instance, stuck to her belief that the oversexing of men was the creation of male supremacy, and remained hostile to sexual permissiveness as being against women's interests (Gordon, 1977, pp. 182–4). More recently, Ann Jones has argued persuasively that the new sexual doctrine promulgated by the new sex 'experts' was an astonishingly powerful instrument of social control:

In place of external rules the new sexual doctrine pressed woman's own desire for 'self-fulfilment' into service as policeman. It enlisted her individual, isolated search for 'sex adjustment' – obscuring the common social and political concerns all women shared. As an instrument of social control sex was powerful, and it worked (Jones, 1980, p. 247).

Dworkin (1981) has also offered some important insights into Ellis's role in normalizing and justifying male sexual violence, by asserting woman's 'eagerness' to subject herself to male power in sexual intercourse.

Support for the argument that sex is an instrument of social control has also come from the rediscovery of female friendships and support networks in the nineteenth century and earlier. Smith-Rosenberg (1975) has attempted to trace and interpret the intensely emotional and often sensual bonds between middle-class women in nineteenth-century America, raising the question of why it was that such relationships were openly expressed and tolerated at that time, but not in the twentieth century. She speculates that in this century 'cultural taboos' evolved, 'to cut short the homosocial ties of girlhood and to impel the emerging women of thirteen or fourteen toward heterosexual relationships' (ibid., p. 27). Nancy Sahli (1979) shows how these networks of female friendship came under increasing stress towards the end of the nineteenth century, when a new definition of what constituted 'normal' female relationships developed in both America and Europe. Love between women, irrespective of whether it actually involved either physical or genital contact, became defined as abnormal, as a perversion – as lesbian. Sahli points out that Ellis was strongly implicated in this process; and that he linked the alleged increase in lesbianism in the nineteenth century to the influence of the Women's Movement, which he saw as 1 developing 'the germs' of lesbianism, by promoting 'hereditary neurosis', and 2 causing a 'spurious imitation' of lesbianism. This 'morbidification' of love between women has been fully explored by Lillian Faderman, so I will not go into more detail here. It is perhaps worth emphasizing, however, that this distinction between 'real' lesbians (in Ellis's opinion congenitally inverted, invariably masculine and often predatory in character), and 'spurious imitations' (i.e. the man-hating products of feminism), is one which is still very much alive today. Faderman argues that the sexologists provided a weapon against love between women at a time when women's increasing independence threatened the social structure: 'If they gained all the freedom that feminists agitated for, what would attract them to marriage?' (Faderman, 1981, p. 237). Sahli also argues that the label 'lesbian' became synonymous with female autonomy and commitment between women because feminism and women's independence constituted a threat to the established (patriarchal) order:

and one way to control these sexless termites, hermaphroditic spinsters, or whatever one might call them, was to condemn their love relationships – the one aspect of their behaviour, which, regardless of their other social, political, or economic activities, posed a basic threat to a system where the fundamental expression of power was that of one sex over another (Sahli, 1979, p. 27).

While I basically agree with this analysis, it seems to me that it is slightly weakened by an over-concentration on the outlawing of love between women, without linking it to the more general struggle around heterosexuality at that time, and the feminist challenge to male sexuality. In the following discussion of Ellis's *Studies in the Psychology of Sex*, I attempt to show that the morbidification of lesbianism is, as it were, only one side of the coin: the other is the male orchestration of female sexual 'pleasure' through the 'art of love'. Together, their effect is to conscript women not only into heterosexuality (and, though I do not discuss this at length, motherhood), but into a form of heterosexuality which is both an expression of, and a means of maintaining, male power over women. As Cicely Hamilton put it:

In sexual matters it would appear that the whole trend and tendency of man's relation to woman has been to make refusal impossible and to cut off every avenue of escape from the gratification of his desires (Hamilton, 1909, p. 35).

Ellis's 'science' of sex constitutes above all an apology for and a justification of precisely that form of male sexuality which contemporary feminists were challenging: a sexuality based on 'uncontrollable urges', power and violence. By claiming that this form of male sexuality was biologically determined, and therefore inevitable, the feminist challenge was undermined and male sexual domination legitimated. I am suggesting, therefore, that the underlying ideology of Ellis's sexology represents a counter-attack against feminism and women's increasing independence; that, in the guise of scientific objectivity and sexual 'liberalism', it reasserts men's right of access to women's bodies, thus reinforcing the social control of women by men and contributing to the maintenance of male supremacy.

The sexual ideology of Havelock Ellis

The *Studies in the Psychology of Sex*[6] constitute the core of Ellis's scientific enterprise and, in Andrea Dworkin's words, the first codification of male sexual values (Dworkin, 1981).

The two main themes which are interwoven throughout the work are these:

1 the notion that normal heterosexual sex is based on a power relation which is biologically determined; masculine domination and female submission are therefore not only inevitable but essential to sexual pleasure;
2 the notion that all forms of abnormal sex are merely extensions of the normal; even the most violent and dangerous forms of sexual perversion are ultimately rooted in 'innocent and instinctive impulses', and thus, it is implied, harmless and acceptable.

These themes emerge from the very first essay in Volume 1, in which Ellis discusses the evolution of modesty. He regards modesty as woman's chief secondary sexual characteristic on the psychological side. He defines it as an instinctive fear, originating in a primitive animal gesture of sexual refusal on the part of the unreceptive female, i.e. the female who is not physiologically ready for mating. Feminine modesty is necessary, according to Ellis, to arouse masculine passion:

the woman who is lacking in this kind of fear is lacking, also, in sexual attractiveness to the normal and average man (Ellis, 1913, vol. 1, p. 1).

It is an essential element in courtship, which for Ellis means the pursuit and conquest of the female by the male which is re-enacted in every heterosexual act, and is clearly to be observed in animals and 'savages', as well as in 'civilized' men and women.[7] The sexual impulse in women is

fettered by an inhibition which has to be conquered ... her wooer in every act of courtship has the enjoyment of conquering afresh an oft-won woman (ibid., p. 3).

He compares woman to a bitch: when in heat she throws modesty to the winds, but when not she refuses the dog's attentions and squats firmly on the floor, concealing her sexual parts. At the same time, however, this is also an invitation to the dog, and in the human male, mixed up with his ideas of what is sexually desirable in the female. Even in heat the bitch, having first chased the dog, may turn to flee, thus appearing to refuse him and perhaps submitting to his embrace only after much persuasion. This obviously implies that sometimes women give the impression that they are not interested in sex even though they really are; and since in women there can be no absolute certainty – we don't come on heat – there can be no way of being sure whether we want sex or not. This begins to bear an uncanny resemblance to the familiar masculine justification of rape.

Essentially, then, modesty is made to be overcome. It is

[an] inevitable by-product of the naturally aggressive attitude of the male in sexual relationships, and the naturally defensive attitude of the female (ibid., p. 40).

Its physical representation is the hymen, the disruption of which is also a disruption of modesty. Here we have the first acknowledgement that the process of courtship may well involve some pain for the female; at which point the second theme begins to emerge – the normalization of the sexual perversions.

The masculine attitude in the face of feminine coyness may easily pass into a kind of sadism, but is nevertheless in its origin an innocent and instinctive impulse (ibid., p. 42).

Moreover, it is an important aspect of sexual desire, according to Ellis, that the woman's 'favours' should be gained by surprise, and not by mutual agreement; similarly, the more modest the woman – in other words, the more frightened she is – the more sexually exciting she is to the man. The exhibitionist, for example, almost invariably exposes himself to 'innocent, respectable girls', and the urolagnist[8] is chiefly excited by catching the young woman unawares in the act. As if to forestall possible objections that such behaviour constitutes assault, Ellis asserts that feminine modesty is itself an expression of the female sexual impulse; the more modest and timid the girl, the more ardent her desire. Indeed, he will argue later, in Volume 3, that even though sexual intercourse may take place against a woman's will, it is usually with the 'consent' of her unconscious instinct, which sides with her attacker against her own conscious resistance.

Ellis's stated intention in Volume 1 is to clear the ground for the analysis of the sexual instinct. His discussion of modesty, followed by discussions of sexual periodicity and auto-erotism, are intended to reveal

the tendency of the sexual impulse to appear in a spontaneous and to some extent periodic manner, affecting women differently from men (ibid., p. ix).

Ellis was one of the first to examine the idea (suggested, apparently, by Olive Schreiner), that female sexual desire fluctuates according to the menstrual cycle. It was an idea that appealed to him not only in relation to women but also in relation to men. He was forced to admit that evidence regarding a monthly cycle in men was inconclusive, but he claimed that there was evidence to suggest an annual sexual rhythm in men. Records of the behaviour of inmates of prisons and lunatic asylums showed that there was a disturbance of the metabolism at certain times of the year which was reflected in the sexual impulse of men and probably of some women. Ellis links this with the more or less universal phenomenon of spring and autumn festivals, reflecting periods of excitement, mainly sexual in character, and often including orgies. It seems puzzling that Ellis should draw on such highly dubious data to support his hypothesis that sexual desire in men is periodic.

Why was it so important? This, I believe, can only be understood in relation to the historical context, that is, to the feminist campaigns around sexuality, and in particular the demand that men could and should exercise sexual self-control. The implicit message being transmitted here is that not only do men sometimes really have uncontrollable urges, but what's more, so do women. The key element in the myth of male sexuality, i.e. that they can't help it, is thereby reinforced, and the feminist challenge undermined.

In this introductory volume, then, Ellis has laid the foundation of his analysis of the sexual instinct, which will eventually culminate, at the end of Volume 6, in a section on 'The art of love'. The sexual urge manifests itself in the male in the desire to conquer the female; her resistance is not real, but on the contrary, the manifestation of *her* sexual urge – the desire to be conquered. In both sexes the urge manifests itself periodically and thus spontaneously, hence blame and guilt are inappropriate. In so far as the female may experience pain, this, being rooted in 'innocent' impulses, is not inherently harmful or problematic. This model of normal heterosexual sex becomes the springboard for promoting both a woman's right to sexual pleasure, and the acceptability of sado-masochism and all forms of sexual activity based on pain and humiliation.

'Love and pain': the legitimation of male sexual violence

The relationship between pain and sexual pleasure is fully explored in Volume 3, the kernel of the *Studies*, where Ellis examines in detail the processes of sexual arousal and orgasm. These he terms tumescence and detumescence, and compares them to the loading and discharge of a gun. The central problem in this process is that tumescence is not necessarily automatic, but often has to be brought about by the most prolonged and elaborate means. Ellis does not explain why it is that the sexual urge is spontaneous, while tumescence is not; nor does he seem aware of the contradiction between the 'uncontrollable' nature of the male sexual urge and the inability to achieve spontaneous tumescence. This raises the question of what it is that men are experiencing when they have sexual 'urges'. As Ellis himself points out, the process by which tumescence is normally achieved is courtship, which, as we have seen, means the overcoming of the female's resistance. This suggests that for men, sexual activity is not merely about sex but about power, and is further evidence of the ideological nature of the male sexual urge. Ellis argues that force is often a necessary part of courtship; and here lies the origin of the close connection between love and pain. Courtship is, in fact, from an evolutionary perspective, a form of combat: it is consistent with the law of natural selection, since it ensures that only the best and most vigorous males succeed in passing on their genes. The very existence of the hymen suggests that nature wishes 'to reinforce by a natural obstacle the moral restraint of modesty so that only the most vigorous male would insure his reproduction' (Ellis, 1913, vol. 3, p. 32). He continues:

Force is the foundation of virility and its psychic manifestation is courge. In the struggles for life violence is the first virtue. The modesty of women – in its primordial form consisting in physical resistance, active or passive, to the assaults of the male – aided selection by putting to the test man's most important quality, force. Thus it is that when choosing among rivals for her favours a woman attributes value to violence (ibid., p. 33).

To give added scientific authority to this view he quotes at length from Lloyd Morgan, who concludes:

Courtship is thus the strong and steady bending of the bow that the arrow may find its mark in a biological end of the highest importance in the survival of a healthy and vigorous race (ibid., p. 34).

The association between love and pain, then, is constituted by the zoological history of the race:

1   the female's primary role in courtship is the playful but serious one of the hunted animal who lures her pursuer, not with the aim of escaping, but in order to be finally caught;
2   the male's primary role is, by display of energy and skill to capture the female, or 'arouse in her an emotional condition which leads her to surrender', and which arouses even greater excitement in him (ibid., p. 69);
3   these two roles bring about the tumescence necessary for ultimate detumescence and discharge, leading to propagation;
4   because both are ultimately seeking the same end, i.e. sexual union, there can be no real conflict, only the appearance of conflict and cruelty;

5   when there is rivalry for possession of one female an element of real violence and cruelty may be introduced – inflicted by the male on his rival, and viewed by the female with delight.

These fundamental elements of the sexual impulse still persisted in his day, according to Ellis, in the masculine tendency to delight in domination, and the feminine tendency to delight in submission.

Ellis's comments on the close connection between male sexuality, power and violence are extremely revealing. At certain points the distinction between the sexual impulse and the impulse to exert force almost disappears:

The infliction of pain must inevitably be a frequent indirect result of the exertion of power (i.e. in courtship). It is even more than this; the infliction of pain by the male on the female may itself be a gratification of the impulse to exert force (ibid., p. 67).

He notes, for example, that in normal men sexual excitement may be induced by reading exciting accounts of battle and war, and that this may give rise to unconscious longings for satisfaction in warlike games such as football and wrestling; he agrees with Freud that there is a sexual element in the playful combat of boys; he argues that the tendency to criminal violence during youth is a by-product of the sexual impulse and may even be regarded as a tertiary sexual characteristic; and he claims that the instinct of cruelty is awakened by the first sexual relationship and often leads to acts such as the torturing of animals or younger boys. Whether or not such observations are correct is not at issue here; the point is that Ellis was determined to prove that the connection between male sexual desire and the impulse to exert force is biologically determined and therefore inevitable.

Equally significant is his insistence that women find sexual pleasure in both the idea and the reality of pain, whether inflicted by them or upon them. The fact that women deliberately arouse the greatest desires in men at the same time as withholding their favours is, he explains, a form of cruelty and power. He goes to great lengths to show how women enjoy being beaten, raped and sexually brutalized, and have no respect for weak men; thousands of women, it appears, write love letters, including proposals of marriage, to convicted rapists and sadistic murderers. He cites numerous examples from anthropology of ritual marriage by capture, in which it is the bride's 'role' to 'pretend' extreme reluctance; according to the (male) anthropologists she really enjoys being taken by force, because if she really wanted to get away she could! He also cites no less an authority than the Kama Sutra; flagellation is recommended as a form of 'play' to increase excitement (whose?) before and during coitus, while the woman, with cries and groans, 'pretends' to bid the man to stop. Ellis goes to extraordinary lengths to 'prove' that women need pain in order to experience sexual pleasure, even if they claim they do not. He argues, first, that pain and pleasure are indistinguishable in women: 'the normal manifestations of a woman's sexual pleasure are exceedingly like pain' (ibid., p. 84). Second, he argues that women's genitals are less sensitive than men's and cites medical texts, which report cases such as the 'nymphomaniac' who had an orgasm when the knife passed through her clitoris, and the 'prostitute', when growths were removed from her vulva.

Pain, then, is not only a 'normal' constituent of sexual intercourse, but essential to sexual pleasure. In men, it is a normal manifestation of power:

to exert power, as psychologists well recognise, is one of our most primary impulses, and it always tends to be manifested in the attitude of a man towards the woman he loves (ibid., p. 82).

He hastens to add that in the normal, well-balanced man, this is always held in check: he only inflicts physical pain on the woman he loves if he feels it is part of his love, and if she likes it. If he is convinced he is causing real pain he is at once repentant. Given that Ellis himself has so cleverly blurred the distinction between pain and sexual pleasure, how the 'normal man' is supposed to tell the difference is something of a mystery.

Ellis is clearly somewhat nervous about the probable reception of these ideas by feminists, as the following quotation shows:

I am well aware that in thus asserting a certain tendency in women to delight in suffering pain – however careful and qualified the position I have taken – many estimable people will cry out that I am degrading a whole sex and generally supporting the 'subjection of women'. But the day for academic discussion concerning the 'subjection of women' has gone by. The tendency I have sought to make clear is too well established by the experience of normal and typical women – however numerous the exceptions may be – to be called into question. I would point out to those who would deprecate the influence of such facts in relation to social progress that nothing is gained by regarding women as simply men of smaller growth. They are not so: they have the laws of their own nature; their development must be along their own lines, and not along masculine lines. It is as true now as in Bacon's day that we only learn to command nature by obeying her .... We can neither attain a sane view of life nor a sane social legislation of life unless we possess a just and accurate knowledge of the fundamental instincts upon which life is built (ibid., p. 103).

One of man's fundamental 'instincts' is obviously to exert power over woman; one of the laws of woman's 'nature' is obviously to experience the resulting pain as pleasure!

Sado-masochism

From here it is but a short step to the normalization of sadism and masochism. It is Ellis's stated intention in Volume 3 to establish 'the normal basis on which rest the extreme aberrations of love', and to show that

indeed, in their elementary forms [they] may themselves be regarded as normal. In some degree they are present, in every case, at some point of sexual development; their threads are subtly woven in and out of the whole psychological process of sex (ibid., p. vii).

The difference between sado-masochism (and most other sexual perversions) and the normal association of love and pain is thus merely one of degree; the love-bite is an example of the transitional stage.

Ellis supports his thesis with numerous examples drawn from case-histories and letters from 'friends', 'correspondents', etc. Space prevents a detailed analysis of them here; most of them concern men, and Ellis admits that there are very few female sadists, and far more male than female masochists. Yet he quotes extensively from the women's letters, many of which express no more than frustration with their lovers' selfishness, anger at men's domination and control of heterosexual activity, and the determination of the women to define their own sexual needs and wants – hardly equivalent to the activities of the Marquis de Sade!

In order to 'prove' women's love of sadism Ellis again resorts to inference from the behaviour of other animals, which he claims to be almost invariably characterized by cruelty on the part of the female towards the male. He argues that, if in 'man' it is the other way round, this is a 'very slight counterpoise' to the female cruelty which has always existed in nature. As Dworkin (1981) points out, he appears to contradict his main thesis – that woman wants to be conquered by force – in order to doubly justify male violence against women by positing a more fundamental female sadism.

Ellis subsequently devoted two whole volumes to the analysis of various forms of sexual perversion – 'erotic symbolism' he preferred to call it – his fascination for this particular topic probably having something to do with the fact that he was himself a urolagnist, a perversion, he claimed, 'which has been noted in men of high intellectual distinction' (Ellis, 1914, vol. 5, p. 59), and is usually, as in his own case, linked to impotence. The study of sexual perversions is, of course, an important aspect of sexology, which I have discussed elsewhere (Jackson, 1981). The main point I want to make here is that Ellis's argument, that the difference between normal and abnormal sexuality is merely one of degree, has become one of the basic assumptions of sexology right up to the present day.[9] It rests ultimately on the belief, legitimated by 'scientific' argument and evidence, that masculine dominance and female submission in sexual activity have biological origins and are thus inherent in all forms of sexuality and sexual pleasure.

Female sexuality and the 'art of love'

The fundamental elements of female sexuality that emerge from Ellis's analysis may be summarized as follows:

1 female sexual desire is as spontaneous as men's;
2 it manifests itself in the desire to be conquered;
3 there may be a pretence of resistance;
4 there is in most women a tendency to delight in suffering pain.

Pleasure in submission to male domination is therefore inherent in female sexuality. How was it, then, that on Ellis's own admission, most women apparently had an aversion to sexual intercourse? The prevailing Victorian view was that women were congenitally sexually anaesthetic, except, that is, for 'fallen' women. This view was attributed chiefly to Acton, who said that 'the majority of women (happily for society) are not very much troubled with sexual feeling of any kind', and considered the supposition that women do possess sexual feelings 'a vile aspersion' (Ellis, 1913, vol. 3, p. 194). Ellis countered this by arguing that women do have strong sexual impulses but that they are repressed, partly because of the failure of their husbands to arouse them, and partly because the element of pain, which is normal in establishing coitus, fails to become merged with sensations of pleasure. The problem with women is that they are slow to arouse; men, on the other hand, are often clumsy and brutal, because they fail to understand the complexity of the process of female arousal, and attempt coitus before the women are 'ready'. Penis and vagina are compared to a lock and key:

a lock not only requires a key to fit it, but should be entered only at the right moment, and, under the best conditions, may only be adjusted to the key by considerable use (ibid., p. 235).

Ellis considered it of paramount importance that 'frigidity' be cured in order to maintain the institution of marriage. He expressed concern at the rising divorce rate; while he agreed that divorce should be easier to obtain when necessary, he thought it important to counterbalance this by increasing the stability of marriage. He strongly advocated training for marriage, not merely to combat ignorance and prevent sexual aversion, but in order to teach women 'the limits of masculine potency', and men the skills necessary to give their wives sexual pleasure. He applauded Ellen Key's suggestion of a year's compulsory service to train girls in housekeeping and infant care. Motherhood, he said, was 'woman's supreme function', and he bitterly attacked the Women's Movement for tempting women away from following one of the most fundamental laws of their nature. 'The task of creating a man needs the whole of a woman's best energies', he thundered (Ellis, 1913, vol. 6, p. 7).

It seems clear, then, that the concern to cure 'frigidity' is part of a more general counter-attack against those elements of feminism which appeared to threaten two central institutions of male supremacy: marriage and the family. One of his correspondents, 'a lady who has written largely on the woman question', argued that sexual coldness was not necessarily to be regretted, in either sex, but Ellis insisted that it was unnatural:

a state of sexual anaesthesia, relative or absolute, cannot be considered as anything but abnormal ... the satisfaction of the reproductive function ought to be at least as gratifying as the evacuation of the bowels or bladder ... an act which is at once the supreme fact and symbol of love and the supreme creative act cannot under normal conditions be other than the most pleasurable of all acts, or it would stand in violent opposition to all that we find in nature (Ellis, 1913, vol. 3, p. 219).

Part of the problem is the apparent passivity of female sexuality: the female's 'reluctance' during courtship is designed to increase sexual desire, therefore she is not really passive. Ellis compares female sexual passivity to a magnet – it seems to 'do' nothing, but really exerts tremendous power. This apparent passivity obscures the fact that women suffer from prolonged sexual abstinence just as much as men. Ellis lists an alarming number of illnesses and disorders caused by female sexual abstinence, from insomnia to 'nymphomania', from menstrual problems to atrophy of the sexual organs.

Ellis's strictures against abstinence are strongly reminiscent of Victorian strictures against masturbation. It is one of Ellis's major claims to fame that he helped to break the Victorian taboo on 'self-abuse', as it was called, and he devoted a whole essay to the subject in Volume 1, showing that it was universal, natural, relatively harmless and could even be beneficial. It also provided further proof of the spontaneous nature of the sexual impulse. At the same time, it could be damaging if carried to excess, particularly in women, by training the sexual orgasm 'to respond to an appeal which has nothing whatever to do with the fascination normally exerted by the opposite sex' (Ellis, 1913, vol. 1, p. 261). Later, in Volume 3, he explicitly warns that masturbation by women may lead to an aversion to sexual intercourse.

How then, was frigidity (defined as aversion to coitus) to be cured? One possibility was hypnosis, already being practised by at least one doctor to Ellis's knowledge, with considerable success. The hypnotist would suggest to the woman that

all her womanly natural feelings would be quickly and satisfactorily developed during coitus; she would experience no feeling of disgust or nausea, would have no fear of the orgasm not developing; *that there would be no involuntary resistance on her part* (Ellis, 1913, vol. 3, p. 240, my emphasis).

Ellis did not disapprove of such a method, but suggested a more subtle means of overcoming the woman's resistance: the 'art of love'. This he considered to be the 'primal foundation' of marriage and the only possible way of ensuring its stability. It was not enough that wives should endure coitus out of duty to their husbands; they must learn to actively participate and enjoy it.

Their teachers were to be their husbands. This might appear at first surprising, especially since Ellis castigated husbands severely for their clumsiness and brutality, conceding that defloration on the wedding night frequently amounted to rape, sometimes even causing serious injury. He borrowed a musical image from Balzac, who had compared the average husband to an orang-utan trying to play the violin: Ellis aimed to transform him into a producer of sweet and harmonious melodies. The instrument was his wife: 'she is, on the physical side, inevitably the instrument in love; it must be in his hand and his bow which evoke the music' (Ellis, 1913, vol. 6, p. 539). It is, of course, quite consistent with everything that Ellis has said about male and female sexuality that the orchestration of female sexual pleasure should be under male control. As we have seen, the male's role in courtship is, by display of energy and skill, to capture the female, or 'arouse in her an emotional condition which leads her to surrender' (Ellis, 1913, vol. 3, p. 69).[10] Just as, biologically speaking, it is the task of the male to overcome the resistance of the female, so it is the task of the man 'to gain real possession of a woman's soul and body', a task 'that requires the whole of a man's best skill and insight' (Ellis, 1913, vol. 6, p. 531). As we have also seen, the capture of the female often involves the use of force. Ellis argues that this creates difficulties for men because although women admire men's strength, and indeed want to be forced to the things they desire, they revolt from any exertion of force outside certain narrow boundaries and it is very hard for men to know when to stop, especially at the moment when their emotions are least under control. In the last analysis, however, force is not really a problem: for, as Ellis points out, the fact that human coitus takes place face to face symbolizes that humans have outgrown the animal sexual attitude of the hunter seizing his prey in flight, from behind.

The human male may be said to retain the same attitude, but the female has turned round; she has faced her partner and approached him, and so symbolises her deliberate consent to the act of union (ibid., p. 554).

Sexology and the sexual counter-revolution

It is difficult to understand how anyone could interpret Ellis as progressive, in the sense of supporting women's right to control their sexuality. The 'art of love' might be more accurately termed the art of possession and control. It is the logical consequence of the model of sexuality that Ellis has constructed, in which power, pain and pleasure are inseparable. I suggest that he presented sado-masochism and similar kinds of sexual behaviour as merely extensions of the normal, in order not only to render them more acceptable in themselves, but also to build them into his definition of normal sexuality and heterosexual relations. He thus provided a pseudo-scientific foundation for the construction of a form of heterosexuality and sexual pleasure through which women could be controlled and male power maintained. The 'art of love' consists in teaching women to accept male violence as inevitable and male sexual demands as normal, to experience submission as pleasure, to 'consent' to conquest – in other words, to 'enjoy' the exercise of precisely that form of male sexuality which feminists had challenged. The morbidification of love between women and the orchestration of female sexual pleasure combined to undermine female sexual and emotional autonomy; and, together with scientific legitimation of the idea that sex and power are inseparable, they constituted a powerful ideology, conscripting women into heterosexuality, and thus re-establishing men's right of access to their bodies.[11] In this sense, Ellis's sexology may be seen as providing a powerful weapon in the male sexual counter-revolution.

By the 1920s Ellis was established as the leading scientific authority on sexual behaviour, and his influence has been considerable, right up to the present day. The best selling marriage manual, Van de Velde's *Ideal Marriage*,[12] clearly owes much to Ellis, and includes a discussion of the association between love and pain which is based directly on Ellis and unequivocally asserts:

What both man and woman, driven by obscure primitive urges, wish to feel in the sexual act, is the essential force of *maleness*, which expresses itself in a sort of violent and absolute *possession* of the woman. And so both of them can and do exult in a certain degree of male aggression and dominance – whether actual or apparent – which proclaims this essential force (Van de Velde, 1977, p. 153).

According to Robinson (1976) Ellis's 'art of love' became the prototype of the countless how-to-do-it sex manuals of the twentieth century, with their emphasis on 'foreplay', or, as I prefer to call it, conquest by manipulation. Even Marie Stopes, who disliked both Ellis himself, and his obsession with the perversions, and whose own marrige manuals emphasized the importance of the woman defining her own sexual needs, regarded him as *the* authority in the field of sex and was very much influenced by him. Indeed, I believe it is his influence which is the major source of the many ambiguities and confusions in her work. Freud may have been the chief architect of the sexual counter-revolution, but I suggest that it is Ellis's work which has had the greater influence on mainstream conceptions of sex. He certainly did much to reinforce the still dominant ideology of rape – that men can't help it and women really enjoy it. At a more scientific level, his suggestion of a continuum of normality/abnormality, taken up by Kinsey, remains central to contemporary sex research; and, as Robinson (1976) points out, Ellis's *Studies* established the basic moral categories for nearly all sexual theorizing, including the recent work of Masters and Johnson (see Chapter 3).

The impact of Ellis's ideas is perhaps most evident in the sex 'reform' movement of the 1920s, which can be seen as a backlash against women's independence and feminism even though some feminists were involved in it (Jeffreys, 1981). Even before the First World War the attack on spinsters, 'prudes' and other varieties of 'sexually anaesthetic' women had begun, not only in Ellis's writings, but in progressive journals such as *The Freewoman*.[13] Stella Browne was particularly vicious in her attack on the spinster, calling her 'our social nemesis', and bemoaning the influence on the Women's Movement of these 'sexually defiant and disappointed women, impervious to facts and logic and deeply ignorant of life' (*The Freewoman*, 7 March 1912, p. 313). In the post-war years, while the hatred of spinsters continued (and the rate of marriage increased), the main target of sex reformers became frigidity, which was apparently reaching epidemic proportions, and was diagnosed not as mere coldness but as sex *resistance* (Gallichan, 1927). Why were women resisting the joys of sex? Could it be that what they were resisting was male control through sexual pleasure?[14]

As Jeffreys (1981) has pointed out, the feminist critique of male sexuality was driven out of the debate on sexuality in the 1920s, reducing it to two 'sides' – 'progressives' and 'prudes'. It remains a central assumption of the ideology of sexual liberation that everyone is either 'for' sex or 'against' it, and feminists who have reasserted the challenge to the social control of women through male violence and sexual 'pleasure' are again being dismissed as prudes.[15] It is surely no coincidence that this is happening at a time when women are reasserting their autonomy and independence from men, and the institution of heterosexuality is once again under threat. The cliché that history repeats itself has some relevance to the struggle for women's liberation. One of the reasons is that men destroy the links with our past, so that new generations of women remain unaware of the struggles of our foresisters. The ideology of sexual liberation, with its doctrine of 'a woman's right to sexual pleasure', has for too long obscured the roots of male supremacy.

Notes

1 The concept of sexual colonization is adapted from Morgan (1978, pp. 160–2), but in no way implies a simple or direct analogy between racism and women's oppression. There are important differences between black women, women of colour and white women, in terms of their experiences of sexual violence, harassment, coercion and control in a society that is not only male supremacist but racist. These differences cannot be explored in the context of the specific historical focus of this chapter, but I believe that the general argument is relevant to understanding the oppression of all women, though not necessarily in precisely the same way.

2 See, for example, Campbell (1980) and Coward (1978).

3 For some recent statements of this position see: *Heresies* (1981), English, *et al.* (1981 and 1982), *Off Our Backs* (1982); and Weeks (1982), who describes the position as 'radical pluralism'.

4 See, for example, Banks (1981) and Taylor (1981).

5 For a detailed analysis of the feminist challenge to male sexuality in the late nineteenth and early twentieth centuries, see Sheila Jeffreys (Chapter 1).

6 Ellis's writing spanned the last decade of the nineteenth century and the first four decades of the twentieth century; he died in 1939, shortly before Freud. *Studies in the Psychology of Sex* were published over the period 1897–1910 (vols. 1–6), and revised in 1913–15. Volume 7 was added in 1928 and new editions were published in 1936–7, with many reprintings.

7 Racism is a pervasive feature of Ellis's writing, as it was of contemporary biology and anthropology upon which he relied heavily to support his ideas. Ellis himself, like many of his

'progressive' contemporaries, took a keen interest in eugenics, the sexist and racist implications of which seem to have entirely escaped him. I hope to deal with these aspects of sexology in another article.

8   'Urolagnia' refers to the phenomenon of men deriving sexual pleasure from watching women urinate.

9   It is, for example, an important aspect of research at the Institute for Sex Research (the 'Kinsey Institute'). See Robinson (1976) and Weinberg (1976).

10   See the above discussion on courtship (p. 57).

11   The term 'conscription' has been borrowed from Sheila Jeffreys (see Chapter 1).

12   Van de Velde was a Dutch gynaecologist, whose *Ideal Marriage* was first published in English in 1928, translated by Stella Browne. It has been reprinted, with revisions, thirty-eight times, and the cover of the 1977 paperback proclaims: 'over 1,000,000 copies sold'. It also reads, under the title: 'The Book Doctors Recommend'.

13   *The Freewoman* was published in London from 1911 to 1913.

14   The social construction of 'the frigide' is explored by Jeffreys (1983).

15   See references in note 3, and a critique by Egerton (1981).

3 Sexology and the universalization of male sexuality (from Ellis to Kinsey, and Masters and Johnson)*

Margaret Jackson

'Science' and the construction of sexual knowledge

The role of 'science' in the construction of sexuality has become increasingly significant throughout the twentieth century. The findings of the sex researchers, generally regarded as 'facts', have filtered from the academy to the outside world through various channels, not least the mass circulation of sex advice literature. The three major landmarks in the development of sex research are represented by the work of Havelock Ellis, the 'Kinsey Institute' and William Masters and Virginia Johnson, all of whom are recognized as having made important contributions, not only to sexual enlightenment, but also to women's liberation (Brecher, 1970; Robinson, 1976; Weinberg, 1976). Ellis's leading role in the establishment of sexology as a science is widely acknowledged;[1] Kinsey founded the world famous Institute for Sex Research at Indiana University, USA, which still continues to enjoy an international reputation for scientific research into sexual behaviour; and Masters and Johnson 'revolutionized' sex research by taking it into the laboratory, where they observed and measured sexual activity directly, later applying their findings in their own sex therapy programme. Many current forms of sex therapy are based on their techniques, as are the trendier and very popular sex manuals (Comfort, 1975).

The sex researchers have always insisted on the scientific objectivity of their work and sought to present themselves as disinterested seekers after the truth. At the same time, however, they have made little effort

*This chapter was first published in *Women's Studies International Forum*, 7 no. 1 (1984).

to conceal their commitment to sexual 'liberation' and have quite deliberately played an interventionist role, apparently unaware of the contradiction between being simultaneously 'neutral' and 'progressive'. From Havelock Ellis onwards all sexology has been based on a position which can be most succinctly described as anti-puritan. Sex is seen as a natural function which should be allowed freedom of expression, and there is vigorous opposition to 'abstinence', 'continence', 'inhibition' and 'repression', all of which evils are attributed to Victorian 'prudery' – associated primarily, of course, with women. ('Abstinence' could be said to be the major sexual taboo of the latter half of the twentieth century.) Most sexologists claim to be in favour of women's liberation – on male terms; but spinsters, 'man-haters' etc. are held in universal contempt, and women in general are blamed for their own and, more importantly, men's sexual difficulties. Despite tokenistic denunciations of the 'double standard', sex research has in fact been characterized by a profoundly anti-feminist stance. Masters and Johnson, whom Robinson (1976) considers have done more to advance the cause of women's sexual rights than anyone else in the last quarter century, are totally dedicated to the maintenance of marriage and heterosexuality. They have attacked feminism as a 'fad' and delcared that: 'fulfillment for the overwhelming majority of women requires an enduring relationship with a man' (Masters and Johnson, 1975, p. 84) – just as Ellis, three-quarters of a century earlier (and also regarded as pro-feminist), scolded feminists for turning women against the 'laws of nature' (Ellis, 1913, vol. 6).

The main aim of this chapter is to show that sex research is no more neutral than any other body of knowledge, and to challenge the claim that it promotes women's liberation. By examining the assumptions underlying the 'facts', and the broader framework in which they are embedded, I hope to show that it is the interests of men and male supremacy that are being promoted in the name of 'science'. The particular focus of analysis is the model of male sexuality – and heterosexuality – upon which sex research is based. I argue that the 'scientific' model of male sexuality is little more than a legitimation of the form of male sexuality which exists under, and is central to, male supremacy; and that in constructing this form of sexuality as 'natural' and 'universal', the sex researchers are strongly implicated in the maintenance and reproduction of male supremacy.

Heterosexuality: the coital imperative

Two of the most fundamental assumptions of sexology are that heterosexuality is natural and that the most natural form of heterosexual activity is coitus, i.e. penetration of the vagina by the penis. All other kinds of sexual activity are regarded as preliminary (as indicated by the term 'foreplay'), optional extras, or substitutes when the 'real thing' is for some reason not available. Ellis and his contemporaries, for example, warned that in women excessive masturbation could lead to an aversion to coitus. Even Kinsey, who delighted in shocking and exposing the hypocrisy of the conventional moral code by augmenting the importance of 'taboo activities' relative to 'normal' heterosexual sex, betrayed a bias towards coitus. Although he claimed that no one sexual outlet was any better or worse than another, whether it be nocturnal emissions, bestiality, homosexuality, coitus or masturbation, coitus was implicitly the standard by which all other activities were evaluated. Thus pre-marital petting and masturbation were regarded as important merely as means to an end – the avoidance of sexual 'maladjustment' in marriage, defined as the failure of women to achieve orgasm from coitus. And despite his liberal attitude towards homosexuality Kinsey believed that both heterosexuality and coitus were more 'natural'; this is shown by his assertion that one of the physiological 'facts' which constituted a definite pressure towards heterosexuality in all animal species and human societies, was 'the greater ease of intromission into the female vagina and the greater difficulty of penetrating the male anus' (Kinsey, 1953, p. 449).

Masters and Johnson, while acknowledging that women are more likely to have orgasms from masturbation, still view it as something women 'revert' to when heterosexual contacts are limited or unavailable, thus implying that it is second-best (Masters and Johnson, 1966, p. 243); and their preoccupation with curing male impotence and premature ejaculation is itself witness to the continuing centrality of penile penetration in heterosexual intercourse. In fact, the very term 'sexual intercourse', which could in theory mean any form of sexual interaction, is in practice synonymous with coitus in everyday speech as well as in the scientific literature.

The primacy of heterosexuality, and of penetration, in the sexologists' model of sexuality can be partly explained by the fact that it is basically a biological model, within which sex is conceptualized as an ultimately reproductive function, a function necessary to life itself. The analogy is consistently made between the sexual appetite and hunger, and even though it is usually qualified by the admission that indefinite abstinence from sex does not have quite the same disastrous consequences as indefinite abstinence from food, the repetitious use of the analogy seems calculated to imply that the consequences of sexual abstinence might be equally disastrous. The biological model of sex owes much to evolutionary theory:[2] coitus is seen as a biological imperative which has evolved to ensure the reproduction of the species. It is argued, with dubious logic, that because coitus is 'natural' it must be pleasurable; if it were not so, reproduction would not occur and the species would die out. Ellis maintained that the satisfaction of the reproductive function ought to be at least as gratifying as the evacuation of the bowels or bladder – 'or it would stand in violent opposition to all that we find in nature' (Ellis, 1913, vol. 3, p. 219).

Masters and Johnson emphasize the dual role of the vagina – in conception, and as the primary means of the female's sexual expression – and suggest, moreover, that the reason that the vagina is so 'effective' as a means of sexual expression is precisely *because* of its reproductive function. Female sexual response, in other words, represents an invitation to mount:

In essence, the vaginal barrel responds to effective sexual stimulation by involuntary preparation for penile penetration. Just as penile erection is a direct physiologic expression of a psychologic demand to mount, so expansion and lubrication of the vaginal barrel provides direct physiologic indication of an obvious psychologic mounting invitation (Masters and Johnson, 1966, p. 69).

Far from suggesting, then, that the penis is 'irrelevant to female sexual pleasure' (Robinson, 1976, p. 154), Masters and Johnson consider the penis to be indispensable in the release of female sexual tension:

The functional role of the penis is that of providing an organic means for physiologic and psychologic increment and release of both male and female sexual tensions (Masters and Johnson, 1966, p. 188).

Furthermore, their techniques for 'curing' human sexual inadequacy both presuppose and reinforce the primacy of penile penetration in heterosexual activity. Those feminists (e.g. Koedt, 1970) who have welcomed their work as 'proof' of the myth of the vaginal orgasm (and hence of the irrelevance of penile penetration to female sexual pleasure) have, in my view, seriously misunderstood their purpose, which is to cement heterosexuality and marriage through the 'pleasure bond' of coitus.

According to the biological model, then, the primacy of penetration follows from viewing sex as ultimately a reproductive function. On the other hand, it could be argued that viewing sex as a reproductive function follows from the male supremacist assumption of the primacy of the penis. That male-defined sex research should be based on such an assumption is hardly surprising. What *is* surprising, however, is that so many feminists have also been blinkered by the ideology of the coital imperative, an ideology which I believe lies at the root of many of the ambiguities and contradictions in feminist debates around sexuality, past and present. One example concerns the 'separation of sex from reproduction' which appears to be taking place during the twentieth century, and which has been acclaimed by both feminists and sexologists as liberating for women (e.g. Mitchell, 1971; Whiting, 1972; Rowbotham, 1977; Lerner, 1975; Firestone, 1979; Barrett, 1980). Apart from the fact that nearly all contraceptive methods are either unpleasant, unreliable, or actually a danger to women's health, the notion of separating sex from reproduction itself assumes that 'sex' is synonymous with coitus. This assumption is both male supremacist and biologistic, since it implies that in the past, 'having sex' inevitably meant having babies. This assumes first that 'sex' means heterosexuality, and second that the 'natural' means of heterosexual expression is coitus. In the absence of contraception, therefore, the only way to avoid having babies is to avoid having 'sex', i.e. coitus, which is allegedly harmful because it means 'repressing' a 'natural instinct'.

Such an analysis automatically rules out the possibility that our foremothers engaged in sexual practices with other women, or in non-coital sexual expression with men, and practised coitus only for the purposes of reproduction. There is no space to develop this point further here, though it demands extensive discussion, as I believe it to be crucial in understanding heterosexuality and its role in the maintenance of male supremacy. Here I can only indicate the contradiction, in acclaiming, on the one hand, the 'separation of sex from reproduction', while on the other regarding sex as essentially a reproductive function; a contradiction which seems to stem from a failure, by many feminists as well as most sexologists, to question male definitions of 'sex', based on the coital imperative and the primacy of the penis.

The universalization of male sexuality: the essentialist model

Sex research has always presupposed the existence of a basic sex 'drive' or 'instinct' which is biologically inherent but mediated by social and cultural factors. The relative importance assigned to biology or culture varies according to the individual researcher, and on the whole the twentieth century has seen a general trend towards greater emphasis on cultural factors. Kinsey, for example, stressed the importance of conditioning, and Masters and Johnson regard the sexual function as 'infinitely malleable'. Nevertheless the model, which has been variously described as an 'essentialist model', a 'natural model', and a 'hydraulic model', remains fundamentally the same. Sex is conceptualized as a natural urge or drive, dependent on internal, biological factors, such as hormones, but capable of being triggered off by external stimuli. The erotic stimulus, which can be almost anything, but is usually a member of the opposite sex, triggers man's (sic) deep-seated sexual impulse, which in turn provokes sexual response. I say 'man' because I believe that in this model sexuality is conceptualized as essentially male; in other words, that sexology takes as given the particular form of male sexuality that exists under male supremacy, and attempts to universalize it so that it becomes the model of sexuality in general.

Characteristic of this model is the assumption that there exists in every individual a given amount of sexual energy which builds up over time and sooner or later demands release. The amount varies according to the individual's biological constitution – some are more 'highly sexed' than others – and is basically not under individual control. Men are generally regarded as having a greater 'sex drive' then women, though most modern sexologists now dispute this, and some claim the opposite is the case (Sherfey, 1972). The model thus reflects and reinforces the male supremacist notion that the (male) sexual urge is either uncontrollable or, if repressed, causes neurosis or finds an outlet in sex crimes.

Kinsey's central concept of sexual 'outlet', together with his concern for the plight of the young male, illustrate these points very well. 'Sexual outlet' refers to the source of orgasm, the chief ones considered by Kinsey being masturbation, nocturnal emissions (men) or dreams (women), heterosexual petting, heterosexual intercourse (coitus), homosexual relations, and intercourse with animals of other species. The sum of the orgasms derived from any of these sources constitutes the individual's 'total sexual outlet'. According to Kinsey, the factor which had the greatest effect on the male's total sexual outlet was age. In males maximum frequencies occurred in the teens and dropped steadily into old age. The high point of sexual performance was around 16 to 17 years, though the peak of (biological) capacity occurred soon after puberty. As Kinsey saw it, the problem was that this pattern conflicted with social custom: during the last hundred years or so, greater moral suppression and increasing delay in the age of marriage had combined to make the problem of sexual adjustment very acute for the young male, in that he was denied the regular sexual outlet provided for older men by marriage.

In spite of Kinsey's claims to scientific objectivity it is not difficult to see where his sympathies lie; sex 'reform' for him would mean increasing the number of legitimate sexual outlets – preferably coital – of the young male. One major stumbling block to such reform, however, was women:

As mothers, as school teachers, and as voting citizens, women are primarily responsible for the care of these boys; and, to a large degree, they are the ones who control moral codes, schedules for sex education, campaigns for law enforcement, and programs for combating what is called juvenile delinquency. It is obviously impossible for a majority of these women to understand the problem that the boy faces in being constantly aroused and regularly involved with his normal biologic reactions (Kinsey, 1948, p. 233).

Kinsey evidently regarded women as a threat to the uninhibited expression of male sexual 'needs'; a potential if not actual force for the control of male sexuality.

Kinsey's account of the nature of the sex drive is ambiguous: at times it seems to be clearly biological in origin, but elsewhere he treats it as a result of conditioning, i.e. as a learned response to external stimuli. If male sexual response were *only* the result of conditioning, the implications would be quite radical, since the conditioned response could easily be extinguished by means of behaviour therapy. In Kinsey's model, however, the conditioning is underpinned by a more fundamental biological drive, which is incapable of extinction. The male's 'conditionability' merely makes him that much more incapable of controlling his sexual urges, since he is the victim, not only of his biology, but of 'ever-present' erotic stimuli in the world around him, i.e. women – their bodies, their clothing, their images in films, magazines, advertising (Kinsey, 1948, p. 217). Women, on the other hand, are less 'conditionable' then men; thus Kinsey was able to legitimize the sexual double standard by grounding it in 'real psychological differences' between the sexes. As the final turn in the anti-feminist screw he speculated that these differences might ultimately reflect differences in the cerebral cortex: in other words, there might be a distinct, female brain – which would make the psychological differences biological after all! (Kinsey, 1953; p. 712).

In contrast to Kinsey, Masters and Johnson have been criticized for their 'female bias'; Robinson (1976) claims that their 'feminism' leads them to present sexual response as essentially female, while the male's pattern is seen as 'different'. It is true that they characterize female sexual capacity as infinitely greater than the male's, which is described as not only limited but one-dimensional. The female is, in their opinion, definitely the superior sexual animal, with her multi-orgasmic potential and her wide variations in sexual response. While they do attack certain patriarchal sexual values, such as the double standard and goal-oriented sex, their primary concern with male sexual inadequacy (defined as failure to achieve or maintain erection), and with the maintenance of heterosexuality and marriage by means of continuous coital connection, could hardly be called feminist. Moreover the construction of the female as a kind of multi-orgasmic monster, whose sexual response is described as 'mounting readiness' is surely a reflection of a male-defined and male-centred view of sexuality. Furthermore, their insistence that sexual response (erection in the male, lubrication in the female) cannot be willed, sustains the myth that the sexual urge is involuntary. They seem to view sexual response as a kind of animal stimulus–response mechanism; their therapy is based on the assumption that if the 'right' kind of stimulus is applied, sexual response will automatically be triggered (provided that it is not blocked, e.g. by anger or inhibition).

In Masters and Johnson, then, the model is the same essentialist model that characterizes the work of earlier sex researchers and also underpins the libertarian sexual philosophy which became fashionable during the 1960s' 'sexual revolution' – from women's point of view no revolution at all, since it prescribed unlimited male access to women's bodies by means of penile penetration (see Chapter 4).

Sex and power: the legitimation of male violence

The theme of 'the chase' as a metaphor of heterosexual coitus is perhaps the most persistent one throughout the sex advice literature, and is intended to indicate that dominance and submission are inherent in sexual activity (e.g. Van de Velde, 1928/1977). Ellis was the first to argue that the power relation in sexual activity is a matter of scientific 'fact' and therefore normal, inevitable, and essential to sexual pleasure. He maintained that the sexual impulse manifests itself in the male in the desire to pursue and conquer the female; while female sexual pleasure consists first, in the pretence of resistance, and second, in surrender to the male, perhaps after considerable persuasion or even physical force. Ellis cited numerous examples from anthropology and zoology to 'prove' the universality of sexual dominance and submission and argued that it was biologically determined. I have already argued (in Chapter 2) that the attempt to establish this model of sexuality as scientific 'fact' may be seen as a response to the feminist challenge to male supremacy, and specifically male sexuality, in the late nineteenth and early twentieth centuries. It was a powerful weapon in what I have called the male sexual counter-revolution, in that it provided pseudo-scientific legitimization of a form of heterosexuality and sexual pleasure through which women could be controlled and male power maintained. The 'art of love' was to arouse in the woman 'an emotional condition which leads her to surrender' (Ellis, 1913, vol. 3, p. 69). This, in a sense, is what the sex manuals have been attempting to do ever since. Even Marie Stopes saw the man as 'still essentially the hunter, the one who experiences the desires and thrills of the chase' (Stopes 1918, p. 70).

Kinsey, too, believed that the greater submissiveness of the female and the greater aggressiveness of the male were ultimately biological 'facts' which constituted a pressure towards heterosexuality; and though the metaphor of the chase has been toned down considerably in recent years, there are still echoes of it:

You see, if we take a girl with a basically traditional background, we can be almost certain that one of the things that turns her on is being pursued. The chase is delightful, and it has erotic value for her because being pursued intensifies her sense of herself as a *female person* (Masters and Johnson, 1975, p. 74).

To be fair, Masters and Johnson make it clear that they prefer a more 'equal', democratic mode, and the trendier sex manuals now stress the desirability of both partners being 'active', taking the initiative, and practising role reversal. The notion that power is inherent in sexual activity, and that this is biologically determined, is still, however, very much alive in the sex researchers' analysis of the relationship between sex and violence.

While they are usually careful to state that they do not condone sexual violence, they constantly trivialize its effects on women, or suggest that the women provoked it or even wanted and enjoyed it. The notion of provocation, of course, fits in nicely with the model of sex as a biological urge, triggered by an erotic stimulus – woman. And the idea that women want and enjoy sexual violence can easily be legitimated by arguing, as Ellis did, that pain and submission are essential to female sexual pleasure. He also argued, following Freud, that in cases of rape, although coitus might take place against the woman's will, it was usually with the 'consent' of her own unconscious instinct (Ellis, 1913, vol. 3).

One of Kinsey's preoccupations was the sexual abuse of girls by older men, which concerned him not because of the harm to the girls but because of the injustice to the men, many of whom, he argued, were impotent and no longer interested in coitus, yet were serving time in prison for child molesting and attempted rape:

Many small girls reflect the public hysteria over the prospect of 'being touched' by a strange person, and many a child, who has no idea at all of the mechanics of sexual intercourse, interprets affection and simple caressing, from anyone except her own parents, as attempts at rape (Kinsey, 1948, p. 238).

He provided scientific legitimation of the influential liberal view that more harm is done to the child by parental reaction than by the offender's behaviour. Once again the poor male appears as the victim, while the damage to the girl is trivialized:

A small portion had been seriously disturbed; but in most instances the reported fright was nearer the level that children will show when they see insects, spiders, or objects against which they have been adversely conditioned... (Kinsey, 1953, p. 121).

Flashing, too, was explained by arguing that the man merely exposes himself because he believes that his arousal will arouse her. Kinsey conceded that he might *occasionally* be aroused by the woman's fear; but maintained that usually, the fact that he has an erection *before* she sees him 'proves' that he is merely anticipating her arousal! Ellis would seem to have been nearer the mark, however, when he said that the exhibitionist feels he has effected a psychic defloration.

The normalization of sexual 'perversions'

The relationship between sex and violence has also been explored through the study of the sexual 'perversions', which Ellis analysed at length, and has always been integral to the work of the Kinsey Institute. It is based on the assumption that dominance and submission are biologically inherent in 'normal' sex, and that the 'perversions' are merely extensions of the normal. The concept of a continuum of sexuality, implicit in Ellis and explicitly developed by Kinsey in relation to his work on homosexuality, has been used by subsequent researchers to argue that the difference between normal and abnormal sexual practices is merely one of degree, and that any cut-off point between them is therefore arbitrary and culturally determined. What is considered normal in one culture may well be defined as abnormal in another, and vice versa. Ellis, for example, maintained that coprolagnia[3] was grounded in the 'universally appreciated attraction' of the female buttocks, while Gebhard[4] claimed that varying degrees of fetishism, voyeurism, bondage, flagellation and sado-masochism were common in most males; only the most extreme forms could therefore be considered abnormal. Both Ellis and Gebhard argued that all 'deviant' sexual practices were rooted in 'man's' primitive instincts and in the universal tendency to dominance and submission in sexual relations. They both based their arguments on studies of mammals as well as anthropological evidence, but Gebhard also stressed the influence of hormones: androgens (male sex hormones) are widely believed to elicit or enhance aggression. Another source of aggressive behaviour, according to Gebhard, is the frustration that is inherent in living in a peck-order society, but he seems oblivious to the logic of this argument, which is that women should, on average, exhibit more aggressive behaviour than men, since most women are lower in the peck-order of male supremacy. Gebhard is ambivalent about the connection between sex and violence: on the one hand he regards it as 'pathological' and 'unfortunate', while on the other he betrays, like Ellis, more than a sneaking admiration for the 'erotic symbolist':

Sado-masochism is beautifully suited to symbolism: what better proof of power and status is there than inflicting pain or humiliation upon someone who does not retaliate? And what better proof of love is there than enduring or even seeking such treatment? (Gebhard, 1969, p. 80)

It is clear, then, that dominance and submission, power and violence are an integral part of the scientific model of sexuality – a sexuality which is at the same time both male and universal. It is visible in those contemporary sex manuals, which increasingly encourage bondage, flagellation, fetishism and the milder forms of sado-masochism (e.g. Comfort, 1975), and is tacitly condoned by the liberal philosophy which holds that anything done by consenting adults in the privacy of their own bedroom cannot be wrong. (This position assumes, of course, that there is no power imbalance between the adults in terms of sex, race and class, and that therefore the notion of 'consent' is entirely unproblematic.) It is also actively promoted by the pornography industry, the central theme of which is that women enjoy pain and humiliation and want to be taken by force (Dworkin, 1981). Sex research is thus strongly implicated in securing the increasing acceptability of a form of sexual practice which controls women and helps to maintain male supremacy. There may indeed be no qualitative difference between 'normal' and 'abnormal' male sexuality; what this suggests, however, is that male sexuality is itself a 'perversion', in the sense that it is constructed as a tool for the exercise of male power.[5]

Breaking women's resistance: the bond(age) of pleasure

the whole (male) fantasy of the highly excited woman has as one of its meanings that the woman herself is an organ; with the penis in her she becomes an extension of it, a reassurance of its continued existence, and a witness to its supreme power (Marcus, 1964, quoted in Weinberg, 1976, p. 270).[6]

The history of the construction of male sexuality is inextricably entwined with the history of women's resistance to compulsory heterosexuality (Rich 1980), and to the form of male sexuality which has been analysed here; a sexuality based on power and irrepressible urges, in which pleasure is inseparable from dominance and submission, violence and pain. During the first wave of feminism many feminists saw that the relationship between sex and power lay at the heart of women's oppression, and their campaigns against prostitution, the sexual abuse of girls, venereal disease etc., as well as the pre-First World War 'sex strike' (see Chapter 1), were all aimed at forcing men to change, to stop using this form of male sexuality as a means of social control. It is not difficult to see how the new 'science' of sexology, promoted by the new sex 'experts' and 'reformers' undermined the feminist challenge by arguing that this form of sexuality was not merely universal but natural; and by conscripting women into heterosexuality and training them to accept and enjoy the coital imperative. As Van de Velde, who 'taught a generation how to copulate' (Brecher, 1970), expressed it:

(women) have to *learn how* to feel both voluptuous pleasure and actual orgasm.... The wife must be *taught*, not only how to behave in coitus, but, above all, how and what to feel in this unique act! (Van de Velde, 1977, p. 244).

Paradoxically, female sexuality has been defined as both different from and the same as male sexuality; on the one hand less easily aroused, more emotional and more diffuse, while on the other hand stemming from the same biological drive. Its 'otherness' has been used to show how it complements male sexuality, and thus to legitimate heterosexuality, while its 'sameness' has been used to legitimate the form male sexuality takes, and to defuse challenge by proclaiming it as genderless, as a kind of unisexuality. To put it another way, female sexuality has been remoulded on the model of male sexuality, so that we are now held to equal or even surpass men in terms of our sexual capacity. Those feminists who have hailed the revelation of the 'suppressed power' of female sexuality as revolutionary (e.g. Lydon, 1970; Hamblin, 1972), appear to ignore the fact that the model of sexuality which underlies such claims is the male-power-model, the same model which in other contexts, such as working in Rape Crisis Centres or campaigning against male violence against women, they would presumably challenge. It is surely not in our interests, as women struggling to end male supremacy, to assert that our 'sex drive' is as strong as men's, or that our sexuality is not 'passive' but 'active', if, in doing so, we accept as given a model of sexuality which appears ideally suited to the maintenance and reproduction of male supremacy.

The opposition to women's refusal to participate in the sexual colonization of our bodies has taken many forms, from defining us as pathological – 'frigid', 'lesbian' etc., to the latest forms of sex therapy, based on the techniques developed by Masters and Johnson. The principal aim of their work is to cement heterosexuality and marriage (which, they insist, is what most women want), by maintaining, improving and extending coital connection, and thus forging a bond of pleasure between the sexes. One is reminded of Freud's view that overcoming a woman's resistance creates a state of bondage in her which guarantees the man's possession of her (Freud, 1977, p. 265). Masters and Johnson's intention is not only to cure frigidity and male erective incompetence, but to maintain coitus at all costs, regardless of its contra-indications for women. They advocate, for instance, without so much as a hint of caution, the use of sex-steroid (hormone) replacement for menopausal and post-menopausal women, solely in order to maintain the elasticity and lubricative capacity of the vagina and hence its ability to endure penile penetration without the pain and damage to the vaginal walls which would otherwise result. It is difficult to understand why so many feminists (e.g. Koedt, 1970) have seen in the work of Masters and Johnson the potential for liberating women from the coital imperative, since they quite explicitly view coition as 'inherent in heterosexual interaction' (Masters and Johnson, quoted in Brake, 1982, p. 189).

On the other hand, marginalizing penetration, which some feminists have advocated as a strategy for reforming heterosexuality (e.g. Hamblin, 1980; Campbell, 1981; Coote and Campbell, 1982), cannot in and of itself transform the social relations of the sexes. Although it obviously has definite advantages for women, there are many other ways of forging the bond of pleasure, as the current debate on sado-masochism shows. Those who argue that sado-masochists are an oppressed minority (e.g. English *et al.*, 1982), and that sado-masochistic practices are quite consistent with feminism (and socialism), base their arguments on precisely the 'natural', 'essentialist' – and male – model of sexuality they claim to reject. Weeks (1982), for example, asserts that this 'explosion' of new categories and definitions represents 'the constant production and reproduction of new desires', the implications of which are 'radical' (Weeks, 1982, p. 306). First, there is nothing new about sado-masochistic fantasies, desires or practices; second, since they represent the epitome of dominance and submission, how can they be compatible with feminism and socialism? Third, the claim, made by Samois (1979) for example, that such fantasies exist in all of us and should therefore be accepted and expressed, seems to be based on the essentialist position that sexual desires and impulses are given, rather than socially constructed, and that it is harmful to repress them. The so-called 'radical pluralism' appears to be old-fashioned sexual libertarianism in a new guise. For feminists the crucial questions would seem to be: how are our fantasies and desires constructed? whose interests do they serve? how can we at the same time accept them (instead of guiltily suppressing them) and transcend them (rather than indulge them or celebrate them)? In other words, we must challenge the assertion that the association between sex and power is inevitable or desirable, and that dominance and submission are inherent in sexual activity and essential to sexual pleasure, whether in lesbian, heterosexual, or gay male relationships.

Future strategies

As Gebhard pointed out:

not infrequently sado-masochistic activity is interspersed with loving and tenderness. This alternation makes the process far more powerful. Police and brainwashers use the same technique of alternate brutality and sympathy to break their subjects (Gebhard, 1969, p. 78).

How many more barricades of resistance will go down before we recognize this model of sexuality for what it is? Sexual response is not a matter of an animal trigger-response mechanism but emerges out of social experience and interaction. In a male supremacist society social interaction is inevitably structured by power relations, and power is actively engaged in the construction of particular forms of sexuality. We have hardly begun to develop feminist sexual practices and feminist ways of conceptualizing female sexuality, but if one thing is certain it is that we cannot start from a model which, like the sexologists', reflects and reproduces both the values and the practices of male supremacy.

Notes

1 Ellis's *Studies in The Psychology of Sex* were published between 1897 and 1910 (vols. 1–6), vol. 7 being added in 1928. He continued writing until his death in 1939, just one year after Kinsey began his

research, which was published in 1948 and 1953. Kinsey died in 1956. Masters and Johnson began publishing their work in the 1960s.

2   It is surprising that while feminists have not been slow to point out the Social Darwinism in ethology and sociobiology (e.g. Janson-Smith, 1980; Bland, 1981; Sayers, 1982), the same tendency within sexology has so far escaped attention.

3   'Coprolagnia': sexual excitement produced by contact with faeces.

4   Paul Gebhard succeeded Kinsey as head of the Institute for Sex Research after Kinsey's death in 1956.

5   For a more detailed exploration of this idea, see Jackson, 1981; for a thorough critique of the Kinsey Institute's analysis of sex and violence, see Dworkin, 1981, pp. 178–98.

6   The publication of this work was sponsored by the Kinsey Institute, though Marcus himself is not a member of the Institute's staff

4 Theory into practice: sexual liberation or social control? (*Forum* magazine, 1968–81)

Lal Coveney, Leslie Kay, Pat Mahony

This chapter was originally sparked off by group discussions of 'The Sexual Revolution' of the 1960s and our reading of Gay Talese's book *Thy Neighbour's Wife* (Talese 1980). Talese's book provided us with an overview of the growth of pornography, massage parlours, erotic communes, and changing sexual mores in America during the 1950s, 1960s and 1970s. It led us to examine in more detail one particular aspect of his study, that is, 'the need for a more impersonal form of sex, which he calls "recreational" or "varietal"'.

This recreational form of sex was epitomized, in Talese's book, by the Sandstone Sexual Commune which was devoted to the 'abolition of "possessive" monogamy' or 'swinging'. Rather than take one American book's word on the proliferation of swinging we decided to find the British equivalent; why it had started and what its effects were on women. We chose *Forum* as a possible source of information on swinging because we found it to be one of the most widely known and accessible sex magazines on the market, promoted as sex education rather than pornographic titillation.

Four of us stormed the bastions of the British Library one Christmas, intending to spend a few hours picking out the articles on swinging and group sex and reading through what we thought would be very few substantial writings on the topic. After two days sitting at the 'restricted reading desk' under the watchful eyes of the librarians, we had only just begun to deal with the piles of *Forum* before us. Not only were the articles on swinging fascinating, but everything else was too, particularly the readers' letters; and we agreed that an overview of *Forum* magazine itself threw up far more broadly interesting questions than a close examination of swinging alone.

Our own reactions to ploughing through over 150 issues of the magazine on that first and subsequent occasions ranged from initial absorption in every word, to boredom with repetition, total hilarity, hysterical giggles, disgust, nausea, anger and, much to our amazement after the first day, a corruption of our senses. In a cafe that evening one of us took the sign 'seating downstairs' to read 'beating downstairs'.

We wondered on several occasions whether readers' letters were describing fact or fiction. Then we wondered why we asked the question. Were we assuming that fantasy is harmless? On reflection we do not believe that what men find titillating is unrelated to their view of women. A man whose fantasy is to rape and torture a woman is unlikely in real life to be free of those images in his relationships with women. Furthermore, our visits to video and sex shops and our conversations with women convinced us that both fact and fantasy are a reality.

The rest of this chapter discusses what we found in *Forum*. For some of us these discoveries were shocking and painful, since we felt that our relationships had in some ways been affected by the practices encouraged by the 'sexual revolution'. What had at the time seemed to be 'liberating' for 'people' turns out now to have been something quite different for us as women.

The 1960s and the 'sexual revolution', which represented a general move towards sexual 'freedom', saw the rise of American multi-billion dollar men's magazines such as *Playboy* and *Penthouse*, presenting 'pin-ups without the hang-ups' (Talese, 1980). These magazines also published readers' letters, a forum in which contemporary issues including personal and sexual problems were aired. Sex was promoted as healthy and fun and an antidote to hang-ups and sexual repressions; but the letters pages began to contradict the 'wholesome' attitudes the literature was promoting.

Forum magazine was first published in England in 1968, and quickly capitalized on the money-making markets opened by the current emphasis on open discussion. It successfully exploited the gap between the ideology and the practice of the so-called sexual revolution: 'Communication is our password and we like to practise what we preach.' The editors saw the magazine as 'the first and leading crusader for the kind of sexual life that you know to be right', with their readers as 'the vanguard of the "silent majority" on the issue of sex freedom'. The specific intention is made evident in the very first editorial: '*Forum* is a magazine about sex .... Centuries of ignorance and superstition, of religious bigotry and social taboos made sex a dirty word....' While sex in the past has been 'misused by sensationalists and tarnished by its perverters', *Forum* was to bring 'sex in all its aspects right into the open world of free debate and discussion...'. With not a hint of irony *Forum* launches its crusade with true tub-thumping self-righteousness:

We are living through extraordinary times. Some historians believe that no age in the world has seen such a complete questioning of the social and moral values we inherited. In no subject are the old beliefs any longer held sacred and immutable, least of all in the social and sexual relationships of human beings. How people behave to each other is a private matter; how they feel about these things is a public matter. Much of *Forum* will be written by its readers.... Other pages in the magazine will be by psychologists and doctors, lawyers and sociologists. Out of this interchange of ideas... we will ... be producing each month a handbook of experience which will help to establish new norms in the conduct of human relationships. *Forum* is dedicated to the principle that acts of love are acts of mutual enjoyment between equal and civilized people.... *Forum* is dedicated to the belief that the pursuit of happiness is a human right and this does not exclude sexual happiness and contentment.... *Forum* is dedicated to a hope that when the world of sex is brought into the open with free discussion and is treated with as much seriousness as other aspects of *man's* life, then for millions of people the fears and phobias, the taboos and guilt complexes, the unspoken frustrations and unhappiness might well become phenomena of the past (1, no. 1, 1968; our emphasis).

As with most party political manifestos or declarations of 'human' rights, the surface appearance is innocent enough, with all its pompous language of sincerity and dedication. However, with such an early emphasis on 'aspects of *man's* life', we already have an indication of the contradictions between *Forum*'s stated aims and its practice.

Forum is an important link between the Reichian and Freudian theories of repression, the sexologists from Havelock Ellis to Kinsey and Masters and Johnson (see Chapters 2 and 3), and the growth of sex therapy over the past twenty years. Because *Forum* popularizes the theories of Freud *et al.*, it makes acceptable the sex therapists' stress on practising the sexual liberation preached by the theorists. Conversely, by describing and promoting these practices, *Forum* encourages an uncritical acceptance of those theories of sexuality which centre on repression as a problem. What is even more significant is that this monthly magazine gained a wide distribution and by 1981 was an established, respectable organization, with fifty-two *Forum* groups around the country and abroad, an Advisory Clinic in London and a doctors' seminar group; it was fighting censorship cases and running private training courses for sex therapists. Even *The Times* had approved. In its review of *Forum* in 1973 *The Times* gave praise indeed: it said that *Forum*'s sustained full-frontal assault on sexual ignorance had contributed to its readers' peace of mind and quality of life, that thousands of readers' letters testified to this, and that *Forum* was a social service. By 1974 *Forum* was on sale in W. H. Smith's, which was still refusing to sell *Spare Rib* or *Gay News*.

To sum up then: '*Forum* is read by an impressive number of people throughout the world.... It is a unique socio-sexual barometer and a form of group therapy' (**3**, no. 1, 1970), tackling the major problem of sex being seen as 'dirty'. We discovered that the sexual relationships which *Forum* illustrates and reinforces are the dominance and submission relations characteristic of 'normal' heterosexuality from which in the last instance only men gain; that the sexual attitudes and practices it promotes normalize sexual practices based on the further humiliation of women, and that the 'new norms' it establishes demand not only the willing participation of women in their own degradation but, in addition, their active initiation of it.

We shall be looking at a number of themes which are found consistently in each of the various sections of *Forum*, whether it be commissioned articles, letters from readers or letters/responses in the Adviser columns. A major theme is *Forum*'s concern with the fact that *sex is seen as 'dirty'*. Another is that *women don't understand male sexuality*. There is also stress on *marital variations for the sexually adventurous*. In the 1970s, *Forum* published a lot of material on the 'problem' of *women as MOMS*, or multi-orgasmic monsters. This led us to look at *women's reactions* to what *Forum* was urging on them. We shall examine each of these themes in some detail. In addition to material from *Forum* magazine itself, we shall also be using extracts from publications promoted by *Forum*, in particular *The Sex-Life File* (1977) which contains many letters from *Forum*.

Sex is dirty

One of the functions of *Forum* is to deal with the question of sex as 'dirty', to remove the feelings of distaste and/or disgust which any sexual activity arouses in some people. '*Forum* is a magazine about sex.... Centuries of ignorance and superstition, of religious bigotry and social taboos made sex a dirty word.' If sex is not dirty there is no place for the distaste and disgust which, in *Forum*'s opinion, cripple many 'unenlightened' people's lives. The reasons for horror and disgust are never examined. The following quote is from *The Sex-Life File*, as an example of the sort of dilemmas women have to face when they feel disgust. From our reading of *Forum*, for example, we would not expect *Forum*'s response to provide us with an analysis of the way in which pornography oppresses women.

I always express my views (on sexual topics) honestly except for pornography. In this I feel a bit of a fraud but I wonder if some women correspondants feel the same and are afraid to say so. My husband loves photographs of couples having sex and has a large collection showing every possible position.... He thinks I share his interest but I merely go along with this because we have wonderful sex together afterwards, and because I love him.... Do you think I should be honest with my husband and stop this viewing before we make love? Which would do the most harm, his disappointment with me or my own feelings of disgust? (*The Sex-Life File*, 1973, p. 150).

Forum also works hard to counter the 'myth' that there is a norm of sexual behaviour with anything outside the norm being seen as a perversion. The message from *Forum* is that sex is good clean fun, there are no norms and therefore no perversions as this quote shows. (Note that this contradicts *Forum*'s original editorial claim to be establishing 'new norms'.)

When we are young we think there is a norm in human behaviour, particularly sexual behaviour, and that away from its cosy fireside a few adventurous souls reprehensibly stray. We imagine a central mass of humanity following nightly the strictest canons of procreative behaviour with equally unimaginative wives and dreaming of no other.

When we have grown wiser and have read Havelock Ellis and Dr. Kinsey and received a few score confidences from persons of the most placidly conventional appearance we realise that there is no such thing; but in its place a variety of people who either in practice or in desire, according to their circumstances qualify for one or another (or maybe more) of the hideous names invented by pathologists to classify them – fetishists, masochists, sadists, pederasts, lesbians, inverts, necrophilists, nymphomaniacs, exhibitionists, copraphilists, transvestists and many others (1, no. 1, 1968).

Note the use of 'humanity', when in fact the text means 'men'. Although this quote dates from 1968, this usage is consistent throughout *Forum*, the language of 'people's liberation' is used to mask the reality of what is being promoted, that is, men's power. The message is: 'anything goes', for men. The inclusion of 'lesbian' and 'nymphomaniac' in the list of perversions reveals the crying need for the analysis of sexual politics which the Women's Liberation Movement later provided.

If there are no perversions there is no need for guilt or anxiety, as this letter from a 'happy heretic' shows:

Thanks for enlightening those of us who have been misguided in marital sex by our puritanical forefathers.... When I look back over the twenty-five years of guilt-feelings I endured because I had been led to believe that certain things were perverted, such as cunnilingus or fellatio, it's a wonder I'm still sane. For instance, I like to suck my husband's penis during love play, but was always afraid to have him climax in my mouth. But after reading some of the letters from other women on how they overcame this fear I decided to try it. I fortified myself with a few drinks to get me in the mood and then proceeded to give my husband the best blow job he ever had.... I don't mind swallowing his semen ever since I read in *Forum* the trick of keeping enough saliva in my mouth so that the taste is hardly noticeable.... I hope this letter will help other women who read *Forum* to overcome their guilt feelings so they can enjoy true sexual feelings with the guy they love (5, no. 7, 1972).

Forum defines the problems as based in cultural repression. The solutions they propose involve the exorcising of these repressions through a whole variety of 'challenging' and 'liberating' practices. Their view is that narrow-minded people must be induced to look about and see just how much a sane society depends upon the 'proper' satis action of the sexual instinct in every living creature.

Basically, these claims suggest to us that for *Forum* the problem is women and their reactions. Whether the talk is of narrow-mindedness, disgust, shame, or guilt, the underlying theme is that it is women's repressions that are the problem, women getting hung-up on sex as dirty; people's repressions turn out to mean women's obstructiveness. We have not deliberately selected quotes from women – there are virtually no letters from men on the theme of overcoming men's revulsions. Since it is women who have these problems, it is not surprising to find that *Forum*'s solution is for women to contort themselves in the attempt to overcome their feelings and become 'liberated' (willing slaves).

Mr Wallis of the National Marriage Guidance Council wrote in 1968 that there were unfortunately many women who had been warped by antisocial attitudes with which they had been indoctrinated from birth. He claimed that in many cases they were able to help these women by 'patient therapy' to enjoy marital relations with their husbands. This is nothing new. See the sex education literature from the 1920s to now – how patient does the therapy have to be? This attitude ignores the warping effect of a woman having to bite her tongue as her husband lies beside her enjoying himself with pornographic photographs; or having to fortify herself with booze in order to overcome her disgust, to tolerate her husband's sexual demands and needs while at the same time suffering from the New Guilt. This is how the New Guilt works. Instead of women feeling guilty because they don't want sex at all, or because they experienced sexual pleasure in the days when women weren't supposed to have any sexuality, they now have to feel guilty because they have these 'unliberated' antisocial attitudes towards their husbands' 'liberated' practices. Wallis is not about to give patient therapy to 'these' women to help them overcome the New Guilt with which he is indoctrinating them.

Women don't understand male sexuality

If the New Guilt is not enough, *Forum* will burden women with their responsibility as wives to nurture their marriages. In order to do this successfully, they must learn to understand, accept and accommodate male sexuality in all its various forms.

A good wife, sexually active, will appreciate the need of her husband for adequate stimulation, and so will learn to join him in his erotic adventures ... even if sharing these things with her husband gives her no positive pleasure, the mere act of sharing will be the greatest help (*The Sex-Life File*, p. 18).

The wife's responsibility to conform and accommodate is underlined again and again. One *Forum* reader wrote in telling of his visit to his family doctor who told him that

most men who have been married for a number of years, especially those who are highly sexed, found they had a great urge to break out of the monogamous sexual ties but due to fear, ignorance and respectability, many of them did nothing about their feelings. The results were usually unhappy, sexually frustrated marriages. There was no doubt in his mind that an unsatisfactory sexual relationship would eventually hurt if not destroy a marriage.

I partake of other sexual morsels now without having to lie or cheat. My wife has given me my freedom, I adore her and we now have a happy marriage (**1**, no. 6, 1968).

Another quote, this time from *The Sex-Life File*, points the finger of blame at women if men have sexual difficulties:

A man can only be sexually active if stimulated to erection, and a great deal of married life consists of activities to achieve this. It takes two to make an impotent man, and if a wife has an impotent husband, she has a frustrated, unhappy, anxiety-ridden mate and an unstable marriage. In many cases she is, however, unwittingly and unwillingly, the cause of this impotence.... Little can be wrong between married partners if it leads to the increased happiness of one (and so inevitably both) and does no harm to either (p. 186).

The 'activities' to achieve this 'increased happiness of one' (no guesses which one), the erotic adventures in which the wife is expected to join are, as *Forum* says, 'as diverse as the persons involved'. Because of this, it is impossible to document all the forms of male sexuality to which women are expected to conform. On the one hand there are letters from women about seemingly innocuous activities: one letter begins, 'My husband thinks he is a horse...' and goes on to describe his cantering around the bedroom and the building of a stable in the corner of the bedroom, which is the bit that's worrying her – no doubt because she'll have to muck it out. On the other hand, as an example of 'games lovers play' this letter appeared in *The Sex-Life File*:

I made my wife put on the very tight rubber corset over the large pad of long blunt nails, as these can cause quite severe pain after a time. Over this I put the wide metal belt... I then gave her the long black rubber gloves and over these put the leotard with the front zip but with holes cut out for the breasts. I always put her in her special six inch heeled shoes.... I never let her off without the spiked heel pads as these can be exquisitely uncomfortable after a short time, as she has to walk on her tiptoes, causing a painful ache in her calves, or else she has to bear the pressure of the spikes in her heels. I find it quite delightful to see her wriggle about and keep changing her position as I watch her try to get relief. I put in the two obturators,* the long wide one into the vagina, and the smaller one into the rectum. I use toothpaste as it causes an intense burning feeling in the anus for some hours, and makes her keep moving her bottom in a most attractive way.... I put on her head the black rubber bathing cap and then put the thick rubber head mask on. This one has an inflatable bag that goes in the mouth, and flaps over the eyeholes so that she is in complete darkness and zips from the crown down to the back of the neck. Over this I put the stiff neck collar and then I blow up the rubber balloon in the mouth. This blows out her cheeks hard against the mask, she cannot talk and her saliva dribbles into the mask. Any quick movements will make her heave so she is very quiet and careful with this on. I then tied some thread round her nipples and crossed her wrists and... tied her thumbs to her nipples. The punishment then began for with her standing up I tied a stout cord to the ring on the leather strap that held her stiff collar in place and fastened the other end to the hook in the bedroom wall. I flicked her on the thighs with the whip, then on her breasts, then moved the front or back obturators until she was in a complete frenzy. I can easily make her have a climax by rubbing the vaginal rod up and down and as she writhes and struggles she pulls on her nipples and tortures herself.

Eventually I could stand it no longer so I freed her from the wall, removed the obturators and took her in the back and front until I was exhausted myself. We had to rest for the remainder of the day, but how I enjoyed it and so did she (*The Sex-Life File*, pp. 69–70).

We have quoted this letter at length because it combines many practices which are described time and time again. We could scarcely believe this letter and suspected it to be male fantasy (which would be horrific enough) until we visited a sex shop and saw the range of equipment on sale, much of which is referred to in the letter.

The pressure on women is to 'do it', up drainpipes, tied to the table, with holly or nettles in their corsets, with rings in their nipples or labia, half-drowned in urine, accompanied by blue movies, etc. etc. (all of these are examples from *The Sex-Life File*). To do 'it' exclusively with their husbands is only one variation. The female partner has to join in whatever sexual activity stimulates her man/husband and this often includes sex with other partners.

---

*A device which closes up a cavity (*Chambers' Twentieth Century Dictionary*).

Marital variations for the sexually adventurous

From *Forum*'s point of view there are advantages in 'marital variatons' for both the man and the woman. The man is stimulated by seeing his wife being 'made love to' by another man:

Group sex... provides opportunities for exhibitionism and voyeurism, displaying oneself sexually and watching others in sex acts. Many people subconsciously wish to do these things but would never do it on their own. In these situations where all consent, the yearning can be fulfilled.... Many men need this extra stimulation in order to be potent at all (**1**, no. 6, 1968). [Note the change from 'many people' to 'many men'.]

The man also gains the freedom to 'fuck' another woman without feeling guilty since she is willing and his wife agrees. Remember the man who visited his family doctor and can now partake of 'other sexual morsels without having to lie or cheat'? For the woman, swinging breaks down her inhibitions as part of her personal liberation:

The unwillingness of most women, even swinging women, to have sex with strangers is not only recognised but catered for in New York. The principle that a woman must be wooed before she can be won is as fully accepted by swingers as in wider society. All traditional phases of courtship from tentative social overtures to full emotional involvement are run through in their usual order and at about the usual tempo. But after the first physical contact – perhaps a holding of hands or a shy kiss – has been made, progress is telescoped. Uninhibited sexual activity is likely to follow immediately.

In Chicago, things are different. Courtship behaviour does occur when one couple is trying to recruit another initially. But after that, wooing is dispensed with altogether. At some Chicago parties, for example, the doors are locked at 10 p.m. and every girl or woman staying after that hour is expected to say Yes or No immediately upon being propositioned... several inhibited women noted that release from their inhibitions through swinging had made them psychologically more responsive (**3**, no. 7, 1970).

Swinging also overcomes possessiveness and jealousy by teaching the woman to separate sex from the emotions of affection and love:

I used to be violent and jealous, and have suicidal and homicidal feelings when he dated other women. I still feel jealous when he dates women at parties, and I am left out, but not as much (**3**, no. 7, 1970).

And the benefits for both, according to *Forum*, are that her 'liberated' sexuality benefits him and her; this leads to better sex together and therefore to a happier marriage. It appears that often wives have to overcome their jealousy by swinging and then they are rewarded with the gratitude of their husbands: 'Husbands feel that they have been rendered a boon by the wives agreeing to swing' (**3**, no. 7, 1970). On the other hand, any jealousy *he* may feel can only be pacified by his exercise of 'veto power': 'In order for one partner to accept the outside sexual activities of the other partner, *he* must feel that *he* is in control of the situation' (**3**, no. 7, 1970; our emphasis).

On the whole, *Forum* is ambiguous about extra-marital variations and in its early days tended to publish articles advising more variety in marital sex rather than looking outside marriage for stimulation. But in 1973, *Forum* advertised a book called *4's Company* about a swinging couple in England, and taking the form of an interview.

Question: What about you, Nicholas? Why do you think you enjoyed seeing another man making love to Polly?

Nicholas: I think in my case it was because I saw it as a kind of humiliation that she was going through for my sake. Somehow I was stimulated by the fact that she was prepared to do this – which was clearly against her nature – as an expression of love for me. And at the same time she was making it possible for me to have another girl without feeling guilty about it. So here was I making love to this very pretty girl with my wife not only endorsing it but removing all the natural guilt feelings from it by endorsing it in the most convincing way possible – by committing the same 'sin' herself (*4's Company*, p. 36, quoted in **6**, no. 4, 1973).

By this time the popular press was regularly printing stories on 'wife-swapping parties' and 'key parties'. In 1971 (**4**, no. 11) *Forum* published an article called 'The Dos and Don'ts of Swinging', urging its readers to prepare for the advent of swinging, which was already well established in the US. They gave simple rules to follows, such as:

1   wash
2   don't do it if you're having a nervous breakdown
3   don't risk your marriage by meeting the same couple again
4   do talk about your experiences with your partner.

By 1976, *Forum* was sponsoring local groups – sometimes called sensitivity groups. These were not always successful because of the reluctance of single women to 'liberate' themselves. One writer announced in *Forum* the proposed formation of two sensitivity groups – one for couples and one for singles in the London area. A year later he is very clear about where the root of the problem lay:

I was very disappointed with the response. I had thought that the female readership of *Forum* would be more interested. As it was, only single men applied, but fortunately there were enough couples to make up two interesting groups despite this. To avoid future misunderstandings, I should point out that Sensitivity Groups are not an arena for slick interpersonal transactions. Only those persons seriously interested in human needs should apply.... As a woman you would be no more subject to molestation from a man than any man would be from you... the worst that could happen is that you, a woman, might help some man to a greater understanding of your sex. Such an experience would surely affirm your femininity (**9**, no. 4, 1976).

The refusal of single women to go to these groups suggests that when couples turned up it was very much at the man's insistence. Far from seeing it as a way of liberating themselves, it looks as if single women might well see sensitivity groups as an arena for 'slick, interpersonal transactions'.

Many variations on a theme had been explored by 1980:

Recently my wife and I received an invitation from two very old friends of ours, to something called a 'wife-display party'.... We called ... the couple who had invited us. They explained what was involved: each wife was to wear a long dress, bra, panties, pasties and a g-string – the latter two items would be supplied at the party, if necessary. At 9 p.m. the dresses would be removed, the bras at 10, the panties at 11, and the g-string and pasties at midnight, leaving each wife naked except for her high heels (**13**, no. 10, 1980).

As before, the pressure is on women to make themselves willingly available to the sexual appetites of men. Again what makes it 'satisfactory' is that the *men* are stimulated but now with the extra benefit of legitimate access to more women. Women are made to feel doubly guilty: they have to share these adventures out of marital duty and they cannot react with upset or jealousy at the husbands' exploits for that would not be 'liberated'.

What is striking about the accounts from women readers about group sex is their sexual attraction to other women – in foursomes, they often ignored the men as much as possible. *Forum*'s answer to this is that lesbianism is good training for heterosexual practice and it also provides unequalled voyeuristic excitement for the men. Since women are engaging in group sex in the first place to please their husbands, any lessons they might learn about their own sexuality are masked for them while at the same time their status as slaves within heterosexuality is underlined. This is because *Forum* is marketing a 'liberated' female sexuality which must remain under male control. But by 1973 *Forum* was introducing in its pages the idea of women's enormous sexual potential which of course created new problems.

Women as multi-orgasmic monsters (MOMS)

Masters and Johnson's research had shown women to have a huge sexual capacity (which, in their terms, meant orgasmic staying power). *Forum*, from 1973 onwards, reiterates this message over and over again. In 1973, an article by Barbara Seaman called 'Are women sexually superior?' was published in *Forum* and was summarized by *Forum* thus:

Barbara Seaman argues that women far outdistance men sexually, are insatiable by nature and could have orgasms until kingdom come – if only they knew their potential (**6**, no. 1, 1973).

Forum's attitude to this ambivalent; on the one hand they continue to argue in favour of women's increased 'sexual self-realization' and on the other they seem to fear women as potential multi-orgasmic monsters (MOMS – our term) whose ultimate effect on men will be to render them impotent.

In a letter to the *Forum* Adviser a woman writes that her husband finds her abnormal because

'I'm still using my vibrator and refuse to stop just because he feels it's an insult to his masculine prowess. Men are so sensitive about their virility, how can women possibly be independent but still keep men happy?'

[The Adviser replies]: 'I don't agree with your husband that you are abnormal, but I do honestly think that you didn't handle this very well.... Unfortunately, a man's erection is very easily affected by feelings of sexual inadequacy. These feelings may in time grow so intense that he becomes sexually inadequate in reality.... What I suggest you do is to reach a compromise with him in which a fib or two wouldn't be out of place. Tell him you'll give up the vibrator... then buy yourself another and make absolutely certain that he cannot know when you use it. This very suggestion, I know, is immoral. But for the achievement of sexual harmony, immorality can sometimes be justified' (**6**, no. 1, 1973).

This advice does not quite tally with *Forum*'s advocacy of open and honest relationships, but more importantly, it does not resolve the contradiction revealed by the woman's question at the end of her letter which shows up the threat to men posed by women discovering an independent sexuality. And there is another aspect to men's problem with the sexual appetites of MOMS. A woman writes that her own irregular sexual appetite 'seems unfair to my husband, since his own desires are pretty constant'. The Adviser replies that such irregularity is quite common, as in eating:

Because of their enormous sexual capacity women, however, can 'gorge' themselves more than men... the cure is to make more serious attempts to be sexual on a regular basis. For example, try reading exciting books and to masturbate daily, or at least every other day for a spell. This will impose a good, sound sexual discipline on you and should make you after a time, less variable in your heterosexual drives (**6**, no. 3, 1973).

Once again, when women's independent sexuality is expressed in ways which are incompatible with male demands, it is women who must be totally regulated. For once *Forum* has spelt out the underlying message to women. Men cannot cope with women's sexuality and anything which is outside male capabilities is monstrous.

Much more fundamentally, it was even being suggested that the very nature of women's sexual pleasure had been inaccurately described. Masters and Johnson's questioning of the importance of the vagina in female orgasm inevitably threatened men, for whom penetration of the vagina (ignoring the clitoris) is an essential expression of their control over women (see Chapter 3).

Dr Seymour Fisher studied orgasm in 300 women over five years. An interview with him in *Forum* reveals:

Dr. Fisher tends to believe that the vaginally oriented woman probably grew up feeling that an important body experience must be shared – as sexual pleasure is shared in penile-vaginal thrusting – in order to be valid: that she has, in fact, no right to enjoy her body alone.

In the case of the clitorally oriented woman, this feeling is less influential. She feels greater autonomy over her own body.... Finally, given the choice of having to give up either clitoral or vaginal stimulation, the vast majority of the women in the study chose to give up vaginal and keep clitoral (**6**, no. 3 1973).

This is strongly supported by women's letters to *Forum*: for example a 20-year-old woman who had been married for a year writes: 'Since we have been married my climax has become almost non-existent except when my husband performs cunnilingus on me and when I masturbate myself' (**6**, no. 3, 1973). Or the woman who had been a prostitute for twenty years who says succinctly: 'I'd rather have a head between my legs than a prick anyday' (**6**, no. 3, 1973).

It would obviously have been tremendously threatening to men if *Forum* had practiced what it preached and encouraged men to *fundamentally* change their own sexual practices in order to adjust to women's preferences; this fundamental change is suggested by a psychiatrist who warns that to deal with sexual problems, 'people' will have to change attitudes as well as behaviour. He suggests that:

The masculinity of the male may depend on an aggressivity or dominance in the sexual relationship which is incompatible with the gentle sharing of 'sensate focus', the Masters and Johnson idea of a sexy cuddle (**9**, no. 5, 1976).

In fact there is little evidence that such a change was being demanded or insisted upon. This next quote is typical of *Forum*'s attitudes throughout. A man has written in to say that after five and a half years of marriage, his sex life is unsatisfactory; he tells the *Forum* Adviser that his wife 'was raised to believe that sex is dirty', that 'she tries awfully hard to please me, but she can hardly stand to touch my penis' and although she masturbates and he does cunnilingus, 'fellatio is still taboo'. This is the reply from the *Forum* Adviser:

A good and fruitful way for you to think of her is as a little girl who is perpetually in the presence of her mother. Her mother will punish her for any interest in sex, so she can only participate if she has an 'excuse'.... It follows that situations in which she has no option but to co-operate are those which you should exploit.

Chasing her, stripping her, smacking her bottom, tying her up, raping her, are all examples of situations in which she is manifestly in your power and she cannot therefore be expected to avoid sex....

Your wife, like everyone else, is a 'sex maniac'. All she wants is an 'excuse' (**6**, no. 3, 1973).

Is this what is meant by that first editorial we quoted, where *Forum* dedicated itself to promoting 'acts of mutual enjoyment between equal and civilised people'? Is this what 'sexual happiness and contentment' are all about? It is obvious from the Adviser's reply to this letter that *Forum*'s ideas of sex and the woman's ideas are completely different. For *Forum*, sex necessarily includes penetration and male dominance. Sometimes we are told the problem is with his frustration at the lack of her response and sometimes, as we saw earlier, the problem is the damage done to his masculine prowess by her 'sexual superiority'. So it now seems that the woman is not only responsible for the man's impotence but also for him having a good time. On the one hand *Forum* asserts women's independent sexuality as the cause of men's hang-ups and yet on the other hand denies it when it implies that men might have to change. More simply, it is used as a cause of men's distress but not as a reason for men to change. Women are always the problem and women have to change. Hence, rather than a flood of letters to *Forum* from women celebrating their wonderful autonomous sexuality, we read of women's anxieties and negative emotions about sexual relations with men.

Women's reactions

The common element in all of the letters is that the women are always *reacting* to what men say about or do to them; rather than focusing on their own needs and desires they worry about their partners and this involves a huge range of emotions and practical anxieties. This is in contrast to the men's letters which reflect their near total preoccupation with performance and sexual apparatus.

Women have been made anxious about their body image; their breasts are too big or too small, their vaginas are too slack or too tight, their bodies are too hairy or not hairy enough. One 23-year-old woman writes to the *Forum* Adviser asking if surgery is possible for her because her husband 'has said that my vagina is much larger than those of girls with whom he slept before we were married'. A letter from a husband details his attempts to liven up his seven-year-old marriage:

I tried her with thigh length boots, spike-heeled shoes, long shoulder length gloves, long hair, tight corsets, chains, dog-collars, flagellation [then he saw a shaven headed model].

Within a week I had her head shaved... I even go so far as having my wife's eyebrows and eyelashes off – it adds to the weird effect – and they can all be added when necessary.

I don't think my wife is really too unhappy, at any rate she knows it pays to please, and after one good thrashing never allows a remote sign of a hair to grow on any part of her lovely body. She sandpapers all over weekly (**9**, no. 8, 1976).

In each of the above letters the woman is reacting to the man's demands and it is *his* judgement of what she is or should be that rules her life. If necessary this judgement is enforced by physical violence ('one good thrashing') but in a lot of cases it only takes the man to be critical of her to make the woman feel that she is inadequate; for example, a woman asks the Adviser for help in January 1981 (**14**, no. 1) because her husband likes anal stimulation and fellatio and she doesn't:

He has had a few girlfriends and says they were all right and didn't complain and acted like real women. Please help me if you can (**14**, no. 1, 1981).

Having been made to feel guilty about their body image, or inadequate because their husbands say they are not like other women, women may respond either cynically or with resignation. The main letter in the *Forum* of May 1976 is from a woman who, after an unhappy marriage, and the experience of being raped, becomes reconciled with her husband by taking this attitude:

So this is what the commotion is about, I thought. Really just a nasty little boy on the boil, kidding himself no end, half crazy for it but only wanting a one-off, and almost out of his wits for it (**19**, no. 5, 1976).

And yet having seen this, she feels impatient with other women:

I know to my cost how little it takes once you know the trick to salvage a marriage and at least make a go of it. It just needs some swallowing of pride and some of the generosity that makes a successful pro to keep a man happy (ibid.).

The resignation expressed in the above letter is underlined by the anger and cynicism in this quote from an article by Marion Meade 'Sex – from the wife's point of view':

But I'm supposed to lie spread-eagled on the bed and enjoy 180 lbs. banging away at my crotch. And have an orgasm while I'm at it. No wonder women scratch when they fake passion. It's because they're being suffocated (6, no. 1, 1973).

Whether women react with guilt, contempt or anger, the content of their emotions, and their reaction to male sexuality, are ignored in the pages of *Forum*. That is to say, women are free to express a whole range of feelings, but it is not their very real anxieties which are dealt with by *Forum*. Genuine heart-felt anxieties and fears are skated over so that *Forum* can quickly return to the real business, to please men at all costs. For example, one woman wrote an extremely distressed letter to the *Forum* Adviser about her husband's incestuous relationship with their 12-year-old daughter. The Adviser replied:

I don't wish to condone what your husband did; he should have had the self-control to hold out against provocation which I feel sure your daughter offered him. But I do feel that your best policy is to try to understand not condemn, if your family relations are to get back on an even keel.

And secondly, in many cases of father–daughter incest it is found that the mother is not receptive to her husband's sexual needs. After all, a sexually happy and satisfied man is far more likely to withstand a feeling of desire for another woman (sic) than a frustrated one. You give no information on your own sex life, so I can only offer this as a point it might be worth your thinking about and perhaps discussing with your husband (ibid.).

For the *Forum* Adviser, the problem in this letter is not the woman's distress, nor the girl's safety, nor the husband's behaviour. Rather it is the girl's assumed provocation of her father, the wife's assumed sexual rejection of her husband. The Adviser concocts an imaginary situation, ignoring what the woman thinks is important: for him, in the short term the girl has caused the husband's loss of self-control, but in the long run the wife is to blame because the husband must, of course, be frustrated. Much as the Adviser says that he does not condone the man's behaviour, he offers the assumed sexual withdrawal of the mother as a good enough reason for the father to rape his daughter.

What we conclude from all this is that far from being an 'international journal of human relations, committed to counselling in the interests of both men and women', *Forum* is in fact operating solely in the interests of men. This is underlined by a *Forum* sex life survey questionnaire, published in March 1980. In the section called 'Variations', the questions are oriented to men: voyeurism, obscene phone calls, frottage, flashing, cross-dressing and use of prostitutes. In the section called 'Problems', there are two questions on impotence and premature ejaculation, the remaining seven are mainly for women: frigidity, vaginismus, disgust, guilt, anxiety/fear, inadequacy and low libido.

Sexuality is something men have: problems are what women have, according to *Forum*. The nature of male sexuality, we would argue, is the problem; and the problem of male sexuality is what *Forum* consistently ignores.

Conclusion

We spent many hours reading *Forum* 1968–81, issue by issue. Although we found isolated instances of support for women, and occasionally a plea for more equal relations between the sexes, the overwhelming message of 165 issues we found to be undermining and degrading to women. To this extent, *Forum* turns out to be nothing less than a handbook for men, suggesting a variety of old and new ways in which women can be kept in sexual slavery by them.

We disagree with Philip Hodson who, in his farewell letter after eight years as editor, claimed that *Forum*'s campaign was 'for personal freedom at all levels' and that the magazine has 'stood for decency in personal relations'. On the contrary, 'personal freedom at all levels' turns out to be freedom for men to use women as they see fit, with every encouragement from *Forum* to write it down so that other men can benefit. 'Decency in personal relations' seems to mean men can do all this openly, and without guilt.

In December 1979, *Forum*'s title page was headed with this Havelock Ellis quote: 'Sexual pleasure widely used and not abused, may prove the stimulus and liberation of our finest and most exalted activities.' This claim to uphold a philosophy of non-abuse is sheerest hypocrisy in the light of what is actually contained in *Forum*'s pages. There is nothing 'fine' in being on the receiving end of 'activities' which involve being shaved, beaten and raped. But according to *Forum* the degradation of women 'exalts' men, that the 'finer' men's activities are, the more debased women are. We must conclude that this version of the 'liberation' of men's sexual pleasure can only be at the expense of women.

Bibliography

Assaults on Children (1914), Report of the conference on criminal assaults on children, London

Banks, Olive (1981), *Faces of Feminism*, Martin Robertson, Oxford

Barrett, Michèle (1980), *Womens Oppression Today*, Verso, London

Barry, Kathleen (1979), *Female Sexual Slavery*, Prentice-Hall, New Jersey

Besant, Annie (1877), *The Law of Population*, Freethought Publishing, London

Besant, Annie (1904), *Theosophy and the Law of Population*, Theosophical Publishing, London

Bland, Lucy (1981), 'Its only human nature? sociology and sex differences', *Schooling and Culture*, 10, pp. 6–14

Brake, Mike (ed.) (1982), *Human Sexual Relations*, Penguin, London

Brecher, Edward M. (1970), *The Sex Researchers*, Andre Deutsch, London

Brighton Women and Science Group (1980), *Alice Through the Microscope*, Virago, London

Bristow, Edward (1977), *Vice and Vigilance*, Gill and Macmillan, Roman and Litttlefield, London and Potowa, New Jersey

Brownmiller, Susan (1978), *Against Our Will. Men, Women and Rape*, Penguin, London: first published in 1975

Campbell, Beatrix (1980), 'Feminist sexual politics', *Feminist Review* 5, pp. 1–18

Comfort, Alex (1975), *The Joy of Sex: A Gourmet Guide to Lovemaking*, Quartet Books, London

Coote, Anna and Campbell, Beatrix (1982), *Sweet Freedom*, Blackwell, Oxford

Coward, Rosalind (1978), 'Sexual Liberation and the Family', *m/f* no. 1, pp. 7–24

Dobash, R. Emerson and Dobash, Russell P. (1980), *Violence Against Wives. A Case Against the Patriarchy*, Open Books, London

Dworkin, Andrea (1981), *Pornography: men possessing women*, The Women's Press, London

Egerton, Jayne (1981), 'The Goal of a Feminist Politics ... the destruction of male supremacy or the pursuit of pleasure?', *Revolutionary and Radical Feminist Newsletter*, no. 8

Ellis, Havelock (1913), *Studies in the Psychology of Sex*, vols. 1–6, F. A. Davis, Philadelphia

Ellis, Havelock (1918), *The Erotic Rights of Women*, British Society for the Study of Sex Psychology Publication no. 5, London

English, Deirdre, Hollibaugh, Amber, and Rubin, Gayle (1981), 'Talking Sex: a conversation on sexuality and feminism', *Socialist Review*, 11, no. 4, pp. 43–62 (reprinted in *Feminist Review*, no. 11, 1982, pp. 40–52)

'Ethelmer, Ellis' (Elizabeth Wollstenholme Elmy) (1982), *The Human Flower*, Mrs W. Elmy, Congleton

Ethelmer, Ellis (1893), *Woman Free*, Women's Emancipation Union, Congleton

Ethelmer, Ellis (1897), *Phases of Love*, Mrs W. Elmy, Congleton

Faderman, Lillian (1981), *Surpassing the Love of Men: romantic friendship and love between women from the Renaissance to the present*, Junction Books, London

Fawcett, Millicent (1892), *On the amendments Required in the Criminal Law Amendment Act 1885*, Women's Printing Society, London

Firestone, Shulamith (1979), *The Dialectic of Sex*, The Women's Press, London

The Freewoman, Weekly Feminist Review, November 1911–October 1912; *The New Freewoman*, An Individualist Review, June –December 1913, Fawcett Library, London

Freud, Sigmund (1977), *On Sexuality*, Penguin, Harmondsworth

Gagnon, J. H. and Simon, W. (1973), *Sexual Conduct*, Hutchinson, London

Gallichan, Walter (1927), *Sexual Apathy and Coldness in Women*, T. Werner Laurie Ltd, London

Gebhard, Paul H. (1969), 'Fetishism and Sadomasochism', *Science and Psychoanalysis* 15, pp. 71–80.

Gordon, Linda (1977), *Woman's body, Woman's Right: birth control in America*, Penguin Books, USA

Grosskurth, Phyllis (1981), *Havelock Ellis: a biography*, Quartet Books, London

Hamblin, Angela (1974), 'The suppressed power of female sexuality', in Allen, Sandra, Sanders, Lee, and Wallis, Jan (eds.), *Conditions of Illusion*, Feminist Books, Leeds

Hamblin, Angela (1980), 'Taking control of our sex lives', *Spare Rib* 103, pp. 6–8 and 19

Hamilton, Cicely (1909), *Marriage as a Trade*, Chapman & Hall, London

Heresies (1981), 3, no. 4, issue 12

Hopkins, Ellice J. (1879), *A Plea for the Wider Action of the Church of England in the Prevention of the Degradation of Women*, Hatchards, London

Hopkins, Ellice J. (1882), *Grave Moral Questions addressed to the Men and Women of England*, Hatchards, London

Hopkins, Ellice J. (n.d.), *The Ride of Death*, White Cross League, London

Jackson, Margaret (1981), 'Sex and the experts: male sexuality rules O.K.', *Scarlet Women* no. 13, part 2, pp. 2–5

Jackson, Stevi (1978), *On the Social Construction of Female Sexuality*, Women's Research and Resources Centre Publications, London

Janson-Smith, Deirdre (1980), 'Sociobiology: so what? In Brighton Women and Science Group', *Alice Through the Microscope*, Virago, London

Jeffreys, Sheila (1981), 'The Spinster and her Enemies: sexuality and the last wave of feminism', *Scarlet Women* no. 13, part 2, pp. 22–7

Jeffreys, Sheila (1982), The Sexual Abuse of Children in the Home', in Friedman and Sarah (ed.), *On the Problem of Men*, The Women's Press, London

Jeffreys, Sheila (1983), 'To be roused by a man means acknowledging oneself as conquered. Sex reform and anti-feminism in the 1920s', in Feminist History Group Collective (ed.), *The Sexual Dynamics of History*, Pluto Press, London

Jones, Ann (1980), *Women Who Kill*, Holt, Rinehart & Winston, New York

Kinsey, Alfred C., Pomeroy, Wardell B., and Martin, Clyde E. (1948), *Sexual Behaviour in the Human Male*, W. B. Saunders, Philadelphia

Kinsey, Alfred C., Pomeroy, Wardell B., Martin, Clyde, C., and Gebhard, Paul H. (1953), *Sexual Behaviour in the Human Female*, W. B. Saunders, Philadelphia

Koedt, Anne (1970), 'The myth of the vaginal orgasm', in Tanner, Leslie B. (ed.), *Voices from Women's Liberation*, The New American Library, New York

Lederer, Laura (ed.) (1981), *Take Back the Night*, Morrow-Quill Paperbacks, New York

Lerner, Gerda (1975), 'Placing women in history', *Feminist Studies* 3 (1–2), pp. 5–15

Lydon, Susan (1970), 'The politics of orgasm', in Morgan, Robin (ed.), *Sisterhood is Powerful*, Vintage, New York

Mackinnon, Catherine (1979), *Sexual Harassment of Working Women*, Yale University Press, New Haven and London

Maclaren, Angus (1978), *Birth Control in Nineteenth Century England*, Croom Helm, London

Mahony, Pat (1983), 'How Alice's Chin Really Came to be Pressed Against Her Foot', *WSIF*, 6, no. 1

Marcus, Steven (1964), 'The Other Victorians', in Weinberg, Martin S. (ed.), *Sex Research: Studies from the Kinsey Institute*, Oxford University Press, New York

Masters, William and Johnson, Virginia (1966), *Human Sexual Response*, Little, Brown & Co., Boston, Massachusetts

Masters, William and Johnson, Virginia (1970), *Human Sexual Inadequacy*, Little, Brown & Co., Boston, Massachusetts

Masters, William and Johnson, Virginia (1975), *The Pleasure Bond*, Little, Brown & Co., Boston, Massachusetts

Mitchell, David (1977), *Queen Christabel*, Macdonald and Jane's, London

Mitchell, Juliet (1971), *Woman's Estate*, Penguin, Harmondsworth

Morgan, Robin (1978), *Going Too Far*, Vintage Books, New York

Off Our Backs (1982), **xii**, no. 6

Moral Reform Union, *Annual Reports*, 1881–97, Fawcett Library, London

National Vigilance Association, *Executive Committee Minutes*, 1886–1905, Fawcett Library, London

Onlywomen Press (ed.) (1981), *Love Your Enemy? The Debate between Heterosexual Feminism and Political Lesbianism*, Onlywomen Press, London

Pankhurst, Christabel (1913), *Plain Facts About a Great Evil. (The Great Scourge and How to End it)*, Women's Social and Political Union, London

Re-Bartlett, Lucy (1912), *Sex and Sanctity*, Longmans, London
Rich, Adrienne (1981), *Compulsory Heterosexuality and Lesbian Existence*, Onlywomen Press, London
Robinson, Paul (1976), *The Modernisation of Sex: Havelock Ellis, Alfred Kinsey, William Masters and Virginia Johnson*, Harper & Row, New York
Rowbotham, Sheila (1977), *A New World for Women: Stella Browne – Socialist Feminist*, Pluto Press, London
Rowbotham, Sheila, and Weeks, Jeffrey (1977), *Socialism and the New Life: the personal and sexual politics of Edward Carpenter and Havelock Ellis*, Pluto Press, London
Rush, Florence (1980), *The Best Kept Secret, The Sexual Abuse of Children*, Prentice-Hall, New York
Sahli, Nancy (1975), 'Smashing: women's relationships before the Fall', *Chrysalis*, Summer 1979, no. 8, pp. 8–27
Samois (1979), 'What Colour is your Handkerchief?' a lesbian S/M Sexuality reader, Samois, Berkeley, California
Sarah, Elizabeth (ed.) (1982), 'Reassessments of "First wave" Feminism', *Women's Studies International Forum* 5, no. 6
Sayers, Janet (1982), *Biological Politics*, Tavistock, London
Sherfey, Mary Jane (1966), *The Nature and Evolution of Female Sexuality*, Random House, New York
Sinclair, Andrew (1966), *The Emancipation of the American Woman*, Harper & Row, New York
Smith-Rosenberg, Carroll (1975), 'The Female World of Love and Ritual: relations between women in 19th century America', *Signs*, 1, no. 1, pp. 1–29
Spector Person, Ethel (1980), 'Sexuality as the Mainstay of Identity: Psycho-analytic Perspectives', in Stimpson and Spector Person (eds.), *Women: Sex and Sexuality*, University of Chicago Press, Chicago and London
Stone, Lawrence (1977), *The Family, Sex and Marriage in England, 1500–1800*, Weidenfeld and Nicholson, London
Stopes, Marie (1918), *Married Love*, Putnam, London
The Suffragette, October 1912–October 1915, Fawcett Library, London
Swiney, Francis (1907), *The Bar of Isis*, C. W. Daniel, London
Swiney, Francis (n.d.), *The Sons of Belial*, League of Isis, London
Talese, Gay (1980), *Thy Neighbour's Wife*, Doubleday and Company, New York

Taylor, Barbara, 'Female Vice and Feminine Virtue', *New Statesman*, 23 January 1981, pp. 18–19

Tuffill, S. J. (FRS) (1977), *The Sex Life File*, Mayflower-Granada, London

Van de Velde, Thomas H. (1977), *Ideal Marriage: its physiology and technique*, Mayflower-Granada Publishing, London

The Vigilance Record, 1888–1930, Fawcett Library, London

Weeks, Jeffrey (1977), *Coming Out: homosexual politics in Britain from the 19th century to the present*, Quartet Books, London

Weeks, Jeffrey (1981), *Sex, Politics and Society: the regulation of sexuality since 1800*, Longman, London

Weeks, Jeffrey (1982), *Gay News*, no. 243, pp. 4–5

Weinberg, Martin S. (ed.) (1976), *Sex Research: studies from the Kinsey Institute*, Oxford University Press, New York

White Cross League (n.d.), *Aims and Methods*, White Cross League, London

Whiting, Pat (1972), 'Female sexuality: its political implications', in Wandor, Michelene (ed.), *The Body Politic*, Stage One, London